WHAT IS LOVE?

by
ANITA NAIK

Illustrations by Nick Sharratt

Hodder
Children's
Books

a division of Hodder Headline

All artwork by Nick Sharratt

Published by Hodder Children's Books 1996

10 9 8 7 6 5 4 3 2

ISBN 0 340 65586 0

Printed by The Guernsey Press Co. Ltd, Vale, Guernsey, Channel Islands

Hodder Children's Books
A division of Hodder Headline
338 Euston Road
London NW1 3BH

CONTENTS

Anita Naik lives in London, where she was born and brought up. She never dreamed she'd land her ideal job of writing for *Just Seventeen*, but now finds herself the magazine's hugely popular agony aunt, advising thousands of teenage girls on their problems. Anita also regularly writes features for *Smash Hits*, *19* and *FHM* magazines. As if this isn't enough to keep her busy, Anita is currently studying for a counselling and psychotherapy course and also does voluntary work for the human rights charity Survival International. On rare days off, Anita enjoys sitting in cafes, people-watching. Previous books include *Coping with Crushes*, *Single Again*, the *Just Seventeen Quiz Book*, and *Am I Normal?*

INTRODUCTION

"The Eskimos have fifty-two names for snow because it is so important to them; there ought to be as many for love."

Margaret Atwood

"If it is true that there are as many minds as there are heads, then there are as many kinds of love as there are hearts,"

Anna Karenina, Tolstoy

What is love? Is it roses and candle-lit dinners? Passion and mind-blowing sex? Is it someone you've once seen? Or is it something else all together? If you're lucky you'll already know how it feels. If you're curious, you'll want to experience it and if you're honest you'll know that it's really indefinable.

Love is best described as a rollercoaster ride. It's full of ups and downs and unexpected twists. It has its scary moments, its exciting moments and its slow moments. Some rides are over too quickly and some last way too long. Some are ultra safe and some deserve to be pulled down. Most times, when it's over, we'll feel sick and claim "never again". But once our stomachs settle down, and our nerves stop shaking, we'll realise it wasn't all that bad. In fact, some of it was quite good fun and before we know it we're off again, having another go. For some people the ride is so upsetting that they don't venture another go for years, thinking all rides must be the same. Thankfully they're not. They come in all different shapes and sizes, and as long as you're brave enough to try, you'll eventually find one that's right for you.

So what's this book all about I hear you ask - rollercoaster rides and things that can't be explained? Well, not exactly. While this book can't offer you guaranteed ways to make love work for you, it can show you ways to make love easier on yourself. My friends and I often play a game called I should have known... It goes like this:

"I should have known he was trouble when all his boxer shorts had YES written all over them."

"I should have known it wasn't love when he brought his ex-girlfriend to my birthday party."

"I should have known he was a hopeless case when he couldn't remember my name after our fifth date."

"I should have known he was a loser when he got arrested on the high street at 11 pm, stark naked and drunk."

I'd like to say that these were the exact points when we all gracefully backed out of the above relationships but, sadly, they weren't. And though all our "should have knowns" seem quite funny now, the truth is they only really hit us after many tears and much heartbreak. Often, that's the way we learn about love. We get knocked sideways and discover the truth while nursing our wounds.

Yet, it doesn't have to be this way. There are some things this book can tell you about that will save you an awful lot of hassle in the long run. Things like when to walk away, when to stand your ground and when to speak up. It will hopefully show you that love can be a wonderful experience if you go about it the right way and a painful one if you take too many silly risks. This book may not make your love last forever but it will help to safeguard you from being hurt. Think of it as one of those safety harnesses on a rollercoaster. It may not protect you completely from harm when the whole thing falls down but it will definitely keep you safe during all those tricky twists and turns!

Anita

CHAPTER ONE

WHAT IS LOVE?

No one really knows what love is but it's a subject that has caused much speculation and argument. Some people believe it's all to do with chemical reactions and hormones, others have more romantic ideals about it. Some people don't believe in it and others throw themselves into it with such gusto that they lose sight of what they are doing. The fact is, we're told from a very early age that no happy ending comes without love. Books, films, songs – they all deal with it, and who can blame them? Everyone wants to be in love, after all, it's supposed to make the world go round.

Whether you believe it or not, at some point in our lives we will all want to be in love. Perhaps it's because we have met someone we are attracted to or because we just feel the time is right. When this happens, the chances are we'll start looking for it everywhere we go. Sadly love isn't something we can order on the phone or just go out and get whenever we feel like it. It's a process that takes time, effort and understanding. There will be times when you feel horrible about yourself, terribly lonely and positive that everyone in the world has got someone except you.

If you're waiting to fall in love, you may be reading this book to try and discover how to do it! If that's the case then I have to tell you that I can't offer you any miracles on how to make someone fall for you or vice versa. However I can tell you that if you're unhappy, miserable, fed up, or sad, having a boyfriend isn't the solution to your problems. Boyfriends are not a ticket to instant happiness and love isn't a miracle cure for the things that are wrong in your life.

"When I met Steve I had a lot of problems. I didn't get on with my parents and wanted to leave home. Suddenly getting a boyfriend changed everything. I really loved him because he was the only good thing in my life. Looking back I put too much pressure on him. I always wanted him to make everything all right in my life and blamed him every time I felt bad. I thought it was his responsibility to make me happy because he loved me, now I know I ruined things. He finished with me because he said I had a distorted view of what love really was."

Sam (17)

When you fall in love for the first time it can be hard to known if you're doing things in the right way. If you're unlucky you'll probably find out the hard way like Sam. If you're curious maybe you'll ask around and see what your friends think. If you do attempt this, be warned. When it comes to love everyone thinks they are an expert!

"I knew from the first time I went out with Paul that I was in love with him. I used to tell my friends and they just laughed at me and said I was immature and didn't know what love was. They said love at first sight was a load of rubbish and I felt like they had ruined everything for us."

Karen (15)

Of course, some people do believe in love at first sight, and others don't. The truth is love happens in different ways for different people and once you accept this, you'll see that anything is possible. No two relationships are ever the same and that's why most advice from other people is a waste of time. If you think you're in love and feel like you're in love, don't let anyone tell you you're not! You are in charge of your own emotions in the same way you are in charge of your body and your mind.

Go by what you feel and what you think and you'll soon discover what love is for you!

❤ WHY DO WE FALL IN LOVE?

Scientists believe that the feeling of love occurs when a chemical reaction takes place between two people. Phenylethylamine is the chemical responsible and this is the trigger that sparks off an instant reaction when we meet someone we're attracted to. Luckily, it doesn't happen with everyone we meet so it can be quite shocking the first time you feel it. Usually adrenalin will rush around your body, your heart may pound, your voice may dry up, your stomach may turn over, your knees may wobble and you may even get a silly smile on your face.

"Whenever I see him I go all silly. I grin madly and laugh for no reason. It just happens, I can't control it."

Sue (14)

"From the first moment I saw him I knew we'd go out. I looked at him and BANG! that was it. Love at first sight!"

Jenny (14)

"When we first met, we couldn't stop looking at each other. It was almost as if we were two magnets being drawn

together. It sounds naff, doesn't it? But that's how it was for us."

Tina (16)

Though this initial feeling of love is based purely on physical attraction, don't be fooled in to dismissing it as irrelevant. Though physical attributes aren't everything, a person has to be appealing before he can register in your mind. And like everything else this physical attraction is all part of love.

The strangest thing about Phenylethylamine is that it affects people in different ways and this is why you may fall for someone your friends will have absolutely no reaction to – and thank goodness for that! Imagine if we all fell for the same person, what good would it do us and the rest of the human race? Biologically, our purpose on earth as a species is to reproduce, and the only way we can do this is if we all fall for different types of people.

On the other hand, some psychologists believe we are likely to fall for someone who resembles us. This is because it supposedly makes us feel safe and secure to be with someone who is at the same level of attractiveness as ourselves. This doesn't mean we make a conscious decision to label people as better or worse than ourselves, or consider ourselves "not good enough" for some people. This attraction is subconscious and not something we actively do. It is also not just physical, it includes personality, likes, interests and dislikes.

"People always tease me because they say all my boyfriends are alike. I don't think they are but I suppose they all have had the same sense of humour and long hair, and that's what first made me fall for them."

Claire (17)

Another theory on what makes us fall in love is the Love Map. This a map that each person carries in his or her mind. A unique guide to what you want from an ideal partner. The map is a record of whatever you have found attractive, appealing or unappealing in your life. It includes things like what makes us laugh, what makes us cry, painful incidents and early attractions. All these items are collected together and imprinted on our brains by the time we are teenagers. Everyone's Love Map is entirely different because no two people have the same experience. Some people may prefer tall, long-limbed people who are studious while others may go for shorter, dark people who like to do sporty things. Other differences include the way we like to show and accept affection and this is again drawn from our childhood. Of course, a Love Map may include no physical features and just concern itself with personality traits.

"I never used to think there was any similarity between my boyfriends but thinking about it there is. Ever since the first person I dated at fourteen, they have all been people who don't conform to rules. They may look and act different, but they have this dislike of authority which is just what I admire."

Yasmin (18)

Of course, apart from the physical and psychological reasons for falling in love, there are also the social reasons.

"Everyone I know has got a boyfriend. I hate being the odd one out. They talk about what they do and I get ignored because I don't have anything to say."

TJ (14)

"I desperately want to be in love. I feel like there is something wrong with me because no-one has ever asked me out. I feel like a freak."

Linda (15)

"You fit in more when you have a boyfriend. People like you more and ask you out. Until then they either put up with

*you or keep away from you because they think you are after
their boyfriends."*

Robyn (14)

*"Sometimes, I think I only date so I have something to talk
to my friends about. At the moment I don't like my
boyfriend but I feel I have to go out with him because people
think we're such a perfect couple."*

Liz (16)

Sometimes, you can feel like the odd one out when you
haven't got a boyfriend and this can lead you to date people
you wouldn't date if you didn't feel pressurised. There is
nothing to be ashamed of by not having a boyfriend.
Boyfriends aren't a badge to wear to show how attractive you
are. If you're single and happy then don't be afraid to say it. If
you hate being single then ask yourself: why? There's no
shame in being on your own and if you think there is because
your friends make you feel bad, it's time to talk to them.

♡ Different kinds of love

*"I sometimes don't understand love. I know I love my
parents and my best friend but will it feel the same when I
get a boyfriend? How are these types of love different?"*

Shannon (15)

Love comes in many different forms. There's the love which you have for your parents and the love they have for you. This is called Unconditional Love, which basically means you know they will love you no matter what you do because their love is not based upon anything you do or don't do. They love you because they are your parents and that's all there is to it. It is very rare to achieve this kind of love with anyone else because most other kinds of love are based upon some kind of understanding or unspoken agreement. This is not to say your parents will forgive you and like you all the time. If they did they wouldn't be human. And unconditional love doesn't mean they will let you get away with everything. If they love you they will protect and help you by pointing out when you're in the wrong and when you've been rotten. Of course, there will be times when you annoy them and upset them and they may tell you that. But at least you'll know that they love you regardless.

Platonic Love can occur when your best friend is a boy and you love him but not in the way you'd love a boyfriend. This kind of love friendship can be infuriating because everyone else assumes there is something sexual going on when there isn't. There are people who believe it is impossible for a man and a woman to be just friends and this is rubbish. When I was at college my best friend was a boy. For the first year we were best friends and yet everyone assumed we were dating and gossiped about it constantly. It wasn't true and it was highly annoying. I loved him but I knew there was nothing sexual about our friendship. Eventually our friendship was ruined by the pressure other people put on us to be a couple when we didn't want to be.

If you have a platonic friendship then don't let anyone bully you into thinking you might be in love. It's perfectly natural and normal to have deep affection for a boy and yet not want to date him.

It's perfectly normal and natural to love a girl. It doesn't mean you are gay (unless of course, you have a very strong feelings that you are or know you are). Loving your female friends is sign that you care about them. It's difficult when you're first getting to grips with love to understand that it has lots of different meanings and that not all of them have sexual elements. Some people may find that they love their female teachers or a famous female star. Again this is a different type of love. It is one that is based on admiration and that's all. It's healthy to have positive role models when you are growing up and it's nothing to feel bad about. Look at how many boys admire football players or sports people or popstars – no one says anything when they rave on about them. If you are besotted with a famous female celebrity and people tease you about it, ignore them. If this doesn't shut them up then point out you admire them because you want to be like them, and it's not your fault that they are too immature to understand that.

♡ Crushes

"I have this terrible crush on a boy I know. He is five years older than me and I love him. I know he'd never look at me and I know he's practically engaged to another girl but I love him. It's so unfair – why did I fall for him when I can't have him?"

Maria (15)

The desperation to feel love and experience its joys can often lead us to jump in and try and experience it even before we have met someone. This is usually known as a crush or unrequited love. For most people, a crush is their first step into love and can be a very important learning experience. It allows us to feel those emotions associated with love without

actually having to deal with an actual person. Anyone who tells you you're mad or crazy or not really feeling love, doesn't know what they are talking about. Crushes can also occur for a variety of other reasons. Sometimes, they can help you get over a painful break up or stir you out of a depression. They are a way of slowly getting yourself back into things without actually having to deal with the day to day mundane aspects of love.

The emotions associated with a crush are extremely real, joyous and painful. The symptoms you will experience are very similar to those of love: a feeling of intense devotion, a sense that you could never be happy without them and a knowledge that this person could be your ideal mate. Sometimes the less likely a love affair is to be, the more you may feel, purely because you think you have something special. This is why so many people fall for popstars, actors and people much older than themselves.

Despite the lack of physical contact, a crush can often feel like love. It begins with a physical attraction and swiftly moves onto something deeper. You may find yourself thinking about that person constantly and wishing you were together. It may mobilise you into doing something positive so you can get closer to them or it may make you feel sad, lonely and depressed.

"I am in love with a popstar and really unhappy about it. I have felt this way for a year and I cry every night because I know I'll never get to meet him. I wish there was something I could do to get us together because I know we're made for each other. The other day I read he was dating this girl and I cried all day. If only I could meet him, he'd see I was the one for him."

Linda (15)

If you get to the stage where you think you are being cheated out of a relationship with someone then it is time to put an end to your crush. Crushes are all well and good if you are enjoying them. But if you're crying about it every night and wishing yourself dead because you're not with them, then this isn't love. It's veering towards an obsession and you need to do something about it.

Likewise, if you are depressed and sad because your unrequited love has made it clear he's not interested, then it's also time to end it. It's important to know that the great majority of crushes never become real, entirely because the chosen person is likely to be unobtainable and out of reach.

Ask anyone who's ever had a crush if they remember it and the chances are they'll say yes. This is because crushes always have a very painful element to them. It's frustrating and exhausting to have a one way love affair with no feedback. If you're lucky, after a while you may decide that you want someone real, not an image in your head and a poster to look at. If you make this kind of decision then you can look back on your crush as a positive experience. However, for the majority of people, realising a crush is never to be, is as heart breaking as breaking up with a boy.

"I think one day I just realised that I was never going to meet him. He was an actor and I didn't know him, no matter how many magazine features I read about him. It was a horrible realisation and I felt humiliated even though no one

*really knew what had been going on in my head. The most
painful thing I had to come to terms with was the fact that
he didn't even know I existed and loved him. It made me feel
like everything had been a waste of time."*

Jules (17)

The best way to get over a crush is to talk about it with people
you trust. People who won't make fun of you and will listen
even if they don't understand. Just like any other kind of
relationship it takes time to get over someone you once loved.
Allow yourself time to grieve – this means don't be hard on
yourself. You're not a failure or a loser for having a crush and
you will get over it. In time, when you have a
relationship with someone you know, you'll
realise your crush taught you some valuable
lessons on how to deal
with love and what
love means for
you.

CHAPTER TWO

BOYS, BOYS, AND MORE BOYS

So you've decided you want to be in love and no one's going to stop you. You're going to go out there and find yourself a boyfriend but the question is – HOW?

- ❤ How do you find someone to go out with?
- ❤ How can you make sure he will stay with you?
- ❤ How will you cope if he flirts with other girls?

Then there are the – WHATS?
- ❤ What if he won't ask you out?
- ❤ What if you're the last single person on earth?
- ❤ What if he just wants sex?

And don't forget the – WHYS?
- ❤ Why doesn't anyone fancy me?
- ❤ Why won't boys speak to me?
- ❤ Why does my best friend get all the boys?

The simple fact is relationships and boyfriends are loaded with questions that begin with how, what and why?

If you want to know the answers to these questions, ask yourself another question first – "Why do you want a boyfriend?"

Do you want one the way you want a new pair of jeans? Because it will impress your friends, make you feel good about yourself and prove that you're someone to be reckoned with? Or do you want one because someone's asked you out? Or because you fancy someone?

If you want a boyfriend for the right reasons then most of the hows, whats and whys will answer themselves.

Your answers will also determine what kind of boy you end up with and what kind of relationship you'll get. For instance, if you're after a boy who'll improve your social standing amongst your friends, then you're likely to end up with a fairly shallow kind of relationship.

The simple truth is if you're honest with yourself and can work out why you want a boyfriend, you can save yourself from some of the nastier pitfalls and disasters that dating brings. Once you've worked out why you want to be in love, the next step is to not look at boys as some kind of alien species. You need to accept that they are as sensitive and afraid of getting hurt as you and me, realising this is the first step to understanding them.

Of course, it's easy to imagine boys are completely different from us. If popular stereotypes are to be believed, all boys are sex mad, immature fools. But, contrary to popular belief, most boys aren't looking for some sex goddess with the confidence and cleavage of Madonna. They want a girl just like them, someone who doesn't know all the answers, won't laugh at them if they mess up on their kissing technique and will be supportive when things go wrong.

Bear this in mind and you'll be a step ahead of all the other girls you know.

♥ So, YOU'VE NEVER HAD A BOYFRIEND?

"I am sixteen years old and the only one in my class never to have had a boyfriend. I don't know why that is because I'm not ugly or stupid. I feel like such a failure."

Sharon (16)

"My friends are always talking about their boyfriends. It drives me crazy. I wish they'd just shut up about it!"

Karen (15)

Steve's always buying me things.

Me and Craig have such a laugh!

Andy's a fantastic kisser!

Like getting your period, developing breasts, and losing your virginity, there is no time scale to getting a boyfriend. I know one girl who has dated since she was 12 years old and another girl who didn't start dating until she was 19 years old. Each girl had a different reason for starting when she did, and neither one has had better or worse relationships than the other. In fact, if you saw them together, you wouldn't be able to tell which girl is which. One isn't more confident or prettier than the other and both have good and bad things to say about dating early or dating late.

When it comes to boyfriends you have to do what's right for you and that's all there is to it. Not having a boyfriend just means not having a boyfriend. Nothing more and nothing less. It isn't something to be humiliated over, or feel bad about. When you meet someone who is right for you (and you will) you will have a relationship.

Until then try not to be competitive with your friends over it or feel bad when they go on about their relationships. If they really annoy you with tales of their love life, then there is nothing wrong with telling them to keep quiet about it. Often, people who are in love assume everyone is interested in their love life, and think nothing of telling endless tales about how wonderful it is. Apart from being nauseating and irritating it can, and will, ruin your friendship. This is why you have to say something like, "I'm pleased you're happy but can we talk about other things sometimes?". If you're real friends you can work it out and find a good balance. Likewise try not to turn into someone who moans and whinges about being single all the time. There's nothing worse than sitting around being sulky just because you don't have a boyfriend. It annoys your friends, it annoys prospective boyfriends – and, eventually, it will annoy you.

Being single isn't something terrible to be ashamed of. Lots of people are single – in fact there are 12 million people who are single in the UK right now. The plain fact is, if you can't be happy without a boyfriend then the chances are you won't be happy when you've got one. Boyfriends are meant to be a plus in life not the be-all-and-end-all of life! If you think one person can solve all your problems and make you happy then you're going to be very disappointed when you do fall in love.

If you are currently single and hate it, ask yourself why? Is it because you feel lonely, left out or abnormal? If it is, then stop worrying right now. For a start, there's nothing abnormal about not having a boyfriend. There are always going to be times in your life when you'll be single no matter how many boys you date. If you believe it's abnormal to be on your own, then you're going to end up going out with people just for the sake of it. This is a guaranteed road to disaster. Always be discerning about who you date and never feel grateful just because someone has asked you out.

If you feel lonely, and left out, then do something about it. Join clubs, organise nights out with your friends, and don't sit in alone. There are hundreds of ways to meet new people. Check your local library and leisure centre for details of local clubs and groups. As for your friends, well, waiting for people to call you, and take pity on you will only make you feel worse about yourself. Remember, you and your mates were friends long before any boys came on the scene so take the initiative and make sure you stay friends. This means organising times when you can go out, having a girls' night in, and basically working to stay friends.

If you're happy on your own and have a full life then you won't ever be bothered about being single. Above all, remember, an added bonus to being a happy single person is you'll become a more confident and fulfilled and this in turn will make you more attractive to boys (even if you decide you no longer want a boyfriend).

♡ DIFFERENT TYPES OF BOYS

Just as there are certain types of girls who want boyfriends for the wrong reasons there are also certain types of boys to watch out for. The following are all stereotypes (they can be male or female but we'll take them to be male here). You may not know them yet, but you're very likely to come across them. If you do, beware – and protect yourself.

♡ Mr. Trophy Girlfriend

You can spot this one a mile off. He's the one who always gets highly competitive with his friends the minute a girl comes on the scene. He's likely to arm wrestle his best mate to the floor to impress you and then show you off to all his mates when he's got you. Sadly though, this affair is not about you, it's about him being the best. He's got to have a girlfriend to show that he is successful in all areas of his life. He'll want you to look good, be clever (but not cleverer than him) and speak only when you're spoken to. He'll hate it every time you beat him at something, he'll flirt with your friends and get angry every time you dare to disagree with him.

How To Deal With Him? Ditch him before he destroys your self confidence.

♡ Mr. Can't Tell My Friends

Some boys are notorious pack animals who can't do anything without the consent of their friends. If your boyfriend is one of these it means he'll keep you a secret if his friends haven't got girlfriends. What this basically adds up to is being pushed aside every time his mates come on the scene. Don't bother trying to compete – you'll always come second, no matter what you do.

If his friends know about you, they're likely to warn him not to get "trapped", or bully him into thinking you're changing him. He's also likely to treat you differently when you're alone to when his mates are about. He might even invite his mates to join you when all you wanted was a nice romantic evening. If you're very unlucky, he'll tell his mates all the intimate things you get up to when you're alone.

How To Deal With Him? Either give him a taste of his own medicine or leave him for one of his friends (joke!).

♡ Mr. I Want Sex

He'll grope you, he'll touch you, he'll tell you he loves you then he'll try to get you to sleep with him. When you say "No", he'll try a different tack. Perhaps he'll threaten to leave you, or make you think you're being a baby for not wanting sex. Maybe he'll encourage you to think if you really loved him, you would give in, or tell you that not having sex is making him ill!

He could even go so far as to tell you you're leading him on. The fact is he isn't thinking about you at all – he's thinking about sex and that's all! If he pressurises you this much, what's he going to do when he gets his way? Probably leave you for someone else!

How To Deal With Him? Tell him to get lost!

♡ Mr. Joker

It's a sad fact of life that boys don't mature as fast as girls. You may be at the stage where holding hands down the street is your idea of romance but he'll still be at the stage where dropping stink bombs and farting in public is funny. My friend used to have a boyfriend who thought it was really "funny" to Superglue things down in shops and restaurants. He thought it was a real laugh – but everyone else thought he was a moron

(and they were right!). Being irresponsible isn't funny. It's irritating, embarrassing, and annoying. He may be trying to be funny in order to try and hide his true feelings but if he can't ever be serious then you've got a big problem on your hands.

How To Deal With Him? Come back when he's grown up!

♡ COMMUNICATING WITH THE ALIEN RACE

Just how do you talk to boys that you fancy? If you're anything like the majority of girls out there you probably have a lot of problems with this one. No doubt when faced with the man of your dreams, your voice dries up, your face goes red, and your head empties of any intelligent thought. This is when you're most likely to make some kind of stupid comment that you want to beat yourself up for later. Over the years my first words to boys have been as ridiculous as:

"It's raining!" (As we stood getting soaked at a bus stop.)

"Come here often?" (At the doctor's surgery.)

"Did you know a sneeze can travel at 100 mph?" (To a boy who had hayfever!)

After all of these, I've wanted is for the ground to open up and swallow me whole. Thankfully it hasn't because I've also been on the other side of it and had boys say:

"Oh, so do you work here?" (While I stood folding knickers and stacking them on a shelf in a clothes shop.)

"I think I once got off with your best friend." (After just having asked me out.)

My point is, saying stupid things is something we all do. It doesn't happen because we're idiots but because we're so worried about making a good impression that we panic and say ridiculous things.

One of the first things to do before you say anything is not worry so much. Any boy who is insensitive enough to make fun of something you say isn't worth losing any sleep over. Secondly, it often helps to breathe before you say anything. Voices dry up because our breathing gets so shallow that we literally run out of breath before we say anything.

As for what to say well, that's simple. Boys aren't some kind of alien species, they are just like you and me. Often our imagination runs away with us and we believe we have to say something deeply interesting and amazing to get their attention when we don't. Just be yourself and say whatever you feel like saying and above all give them a chance to take part in the conversation.

The tip here is to imagine you are talking to your best friend/brother/sister. Talk about a topic you know lots about. Television's always a good one, as is school, and music. If you really don't think you can make it all the way through a conversation, take charge and ask questions. This will achieve two things, one it will let him know you're interested in him and two, it will leave him to do all the talking.

Learn to ask open-ended questions, for instance, say "So what kind of music do you like?" instead of "I hear you like Oasis?". Or "What school do you go to?" instead of "You go to St. James's, don't you?". This way they have to talk to you and not just give you a yes or no answer.

Another tip is not to try so hard. If someone is making it difficult for you to talk to them, try and work out why. Is it because they are shy? If this is the case then don't overwhelm them and talk at them. Often we over compensate for people who are shy and this makes them feel worse. Sometimes, you'll be unlucky enough to come across someone who just doesn't try in conversations. He will give you only yes/no answers, and try and make you uncomfortable every time you say something. The only good thing about having a conversation like this is it's a definite sign that they are trouble. And you should keep away.

Above all remember, if they can't be bothered to talk nicely to you then they are not good material for a boyfriend. Good relationships are based on good communication. When two people can talk without any problem then they have a better chance of having a happy relationship.

♡ TEN WAYS NOT TO GET A BOYFRIEND

"I never have any luck with guys and I don't know why. I try really hard and flirt with them. I even ask them out but I get nowhere. I'm not ugly or stupid, and yet, I'm such a failure in love."

Emma (15)

Just as there are many ways to get a boyfriend, there are many ways to put off prospective boyfriends. The fact is boys are just like you: they are afraid of rejection, terrified of the opposite sex – and know absolutely nothing about love. What's worse for them is that they are often expected to do all the running, make initial contact with you and make the move for that first kiss. Can you imagine anything more terrifying or horrifying?

If you're determined to get a boyfriend remember the above and avoid the following. It may not get you a boyfriend, but it will certainly get the boys on your side.

♡ Lie about yourself

I know a girl who pretended she was the biggest rugby fan ever just to get the attention of a boy she fancied. He fell for it, took her to a game and then she blew it by saying she didn't realise players were allowed to run with the ball. That relationship lasted the grand total of one date purely because he thought she was an idiot. If only she'd been herself, the chances are he would have fancied her whether she liked rugby or not. Not being honest about who you are is a guaranteed way to put off a boy. This doesn't mean you have to spill the beans on your deepest, darkest secrets but it does mean you shouldn't tell lies about yourself. If he doesn't like you for who you are then he isn't the boy for you.

You play it safe with clothes? Me too!

♡ Date someone you feel sorry for

Never date a boy because you feel sorry for him – he won't thank you for it. It can be hard to turn someone down, but that's easier than pretending to fancy a boy when you don't. The end result of a relationship like this is he is going to feel totally humiliated, and you're going to feel even worse. It can also be tempting to say yes just because you want a boyfriend but, again, this is a no-no! The only reason to ever date a boy is because you fancy him – and nothing else.

♡ Date someone to attract their friend

Some girls think a good way to get the boy they fancy is to date his best friend. This is a good way to end up with a bad reputation and nothing else. Boys are notoriously loyal to their friends (like you and me) and won't thank you for doing the dirty on their mate. How would you feel if someone dated you just so they could attract your best friend? Pretty angry no doubt!

♡ Act desperate

There's nothing more likely to have a boy run a mile to get away from you than acting desperate. When you act this way, the message you are giving out is "It's not you I'm desperate to date, but anyone". Apart from the fact that this is insulting, it also makes boys feel scared because you are putting too much pressure on them too soon. Desperation often comes from the idea that if you don't get someone soon, everyone will think badly of you or you'll be left out. Try not to think of things this way. Being single means as much, or as little, as you want it to. Don't do yourself an injustice.

pleeeeeeese be my boyfriend!!!

♡ Go over the top about love

I once dated a guy who told me on our first date that he loved me madly and wanted to know if I loved him back. Needless to say, I didn't give him the answer he wanted, and we broke up. There's nothing worse than meeting someone you like and have them talk about love before you've even found out their surname. It reeks of disaster from the very beginning and adds unnecessary pressure to a new relationship. I believe in love as first sight as much as the next person but there's no need to go over the top right away. Give yourself time to get to know them before you start talking about whether or not you're in love.

♡ Talk about commitment

There's a popular myth that circulates amongst boys that all girls want is commitment and marriage. We know this is rubbish but they don't – and it isn't helped by the films we see at the cinema and on television. You can change this misconception by not falling into the trap of talking about what you want from a relationship as soon as you start going out. Go slowly – you've got all the time in the world to work out how to make your relationship work.

♡ Steal someone else's boyfriend

This isn't likely to win you any friends or do you any good in the relationship stakes. Stealing someone else's boyfriend is a recipe for disaster because the plain fact is, if they weren't faithful to their ex-girlfriend, they aren't likely to be faithful to you! If you happen to be unlucky enough to fancy someone else's boyfriend, keep well away until they are single. This way you'll know that they like you for you and not because you were an escape route from a bad relationship.

♡ Be pushy

Being assertive and being pushy are two different things. There's nothing wrong with asking someone out or letting them know you like them, but not taking no for an answer is bad news. Sometimes, people you fancy won't like you back. This may be painful, but no amount of pushing is going to make them change their minds. Learning to walk away when someone is not interested will save you from a huge amount of heartbreak.

♡ Wait around for a boyfriend to arrive

So you want a boyfriend but one isn't materialising. Why? Simple – if you sit at home and do nothing but dream of getting a boyfriend you will never get one. That's not to say you should rush out and search the streets for one but you should do something with your time. Boyfriends have a funny way of appearing just when you're not expecting it and this usually happens when your life is full and happy. Why? Well, because when your life is full and happy you are more confident and relaxed which makes you more attractive. Remember: people like people who like themselves.

♡ Sit back and do nothing

So, you've met someone you like and you know he likes you. What next? Well, you could sit back and do nothing and risk losing out. Or you could do something positive. Girls are notorious for waiting for boys to do the asking because they are afraid of rejection. The fact is boys feel exactly the same way as girls and are just as afraid of being hurt. If you like someone and think they like you, then you have nothing to lose by taking the initiative and asking them out. If you wait it may never happen.

CHAPTER THREE

MAD ABOUT THE BOY?

You've met the boy of your dreams – he's gorgeous, he's funny, and you're sure he could make you happy. You think about him all the time, dream of kissing him, and imagine what it would be like to go out with him. You discuss him with your friends, write his name across your books and lay elaborate plans on how you're going to make him yours. Then your chance comes. You're in the same place, at the same time and better still, he's walking towards you. What do you do now?

Ask him out, ignore him, say hello, crack a joke, play it cool – or turn and walk away? With so many choices, it's easy to make the wrong decision and end up feeling foolish later. If you've done this in the past or in the not so distant past, don't beat yourself up for it. Let's face it, it's hard being mad about someone. It changes our life, our assumptions and the way we feel about ourselves. More importantly, it changes the way we behave. Sometimes it can make us feel good. Other times completely rotten. And that's the way love is: brilliant, amazing and, at the same time, complicated and confusing.

I have a friend called Kate who was absolutely mad about a boy at college. For a whole year, she watched him, lusted after him, and told everyone (apart from him) how much she liked him. She even sent him a Valentine's card. Then one day he bumped into her, and asked her if she had sent the card. Out of embarrassment, she denied it quite rudely – and he never spoke to her again. Two years later, she bumped into him and laughingly admitted how much she used to fancy him. He was horrified. It turns out he's had the biggest crush on her at the same time, but thought she hated him. Even now, she sighs wistfully at the thought of him, thinking if only she had done this or said that, things would have worked out differently.

The fact is it takes time and considerable effort to learn how to cope with the feelings that surround attraction. You have to learn to listen to yourself and not to anyone else. You have to know how to read the signs coming from another person and not let anyone make you feel bad about your feelings. You also have to find the courage to go after what you want. Of course, just because you're mad about someone, doesn't mean they will automatically feel the same way about you and vice versa. But, if you're willing to risk being knocked back now and again you'll be a winner in the end. After all, as the old saying goes, nothing ventured nothing gained!

♡ HOW TO HANDLE BEING ATTRACTED TO SOMEONE

So you've spotted him. He could be tall, short, round, dark, or fair, but you know he's the one you want and what's more he's heading your way. What next? Well, if you're anything like the majority of people out there, your first reaction is likely to be panic, swiftly followed by some odd physical sensations, and perhaps some even stranger thoughts.

"The first time Will came near me, I thought I was going to be sick. I was so scared I would be, that I hid under my desk. For some stupid reason I thought he'd never see me

*there, of course he did and asked what I was doing. I was
so embarrassed."*
Sue (14)

Being attracted to someone can be a weird experience. You
may find that the person you like is on your mind most of the
time, or you feel sick when you see him. Sometimes, your
knees may wobble, or your stomach may turn over. Perhaps,
silly things will come into your head or you may say something
you don't really mean. Maybe, you'll even laugh every time he
looks your way or do something that you'll regret later.

*"When I first fell for Andy it was awful. I didn't know what
was happening to me, I'd never met anyone who could make
my stomach turn over just by smiling at me."*
Paula (14)

*"I worry that I am going mad because even though I fancy
him and make an effort to be in places he is, whenever he
comes over to me I just ignore him or say something rude.
Once he's gone I feel like crying."*
Tina (15)

The fact is we all do embarrassing things when we're caught
off guard and, let's face it, having someone you fancy talk to
you is like continually being caught off guard. It triggers off all
those insecurities and fears. "He thinks I'm an idiot." "What
do I say now?" "He hates me." It makes us feel as if we are
somehow unworthy and whatever we do next will be a
mistake that will never be forgotten. With so much anxiety
behind us it's hardly any wonder that we say and do the wrong
things.

The best way to deal with it is to learn how to control your
panic. The next time you are in a situation like this and you
feel panic rising, remind yourself that the person talking to you
is just as nervous as you. He's just as scared of making a fool
out of himself, just as afraid of embarrassing himself, and just
as worried that you'll notice that spot on his chin.

What's more, if he's so worried about all those things, he can't possibly notice all the things you're worried about – so you can relax. Once he notices you're relaxed, he'll hopefully relax too and the conversation will become easier.

While this won't cure your panic, it will keep it at bay until the worst has passed. And even if the worst doesn't pass, and you do happen to do something embarrassing, all is not lost. There are a multitude of ways to salvage any fumbled opening.

THE ART OF FLIRTING

"Flirting is easy. All you have to do is smile a lot and look them in the eye. Sometime, I act like I'm very shy and sweet, and other times I'm more jokey. It depends on the guy I'm trying to get. You have to see what they're like first and then act the right way for them."

Sue (15)

"When guys are joking with me or teasing me I just go along with it and laugh. I don't realise they are flirting and so I never get the message that they are interested."

Paula (15)

"I'm not too sure how to flirt but my friend is an expert at it. She bats her eye lashes, giggles and goes all stupid with every boy she meets. I just can't be like that."

Charlotte (15)

Flirting is a difficult concept, go too far and people may accuse you of being sexually threatening. Do too little and people may think you're not interested. We all flirt in different ways, some girls can do it without thinking, others have more of a struggle. I have a friend who literally (as she says) "works a room". Basically, this means the minute she spots a boy she changes her whole persona. Her voice goes deeper, she wiggles her hips as she walks and she flicks her hair all over the place. Unfortunately for her, though she has flirting down to a fine art, her behaviour annoys all her female friends and frightens off most prospective boyfriends!

Trying too hard is as bad as not trying at all. Of course, it's difficult not to be self-conscious when you fancy someone. But not being yourself is silly because, unless you can keep up a fake act forever, a boy will soon discover who you really are.

Flirting is in fact a fine art. It's a way of letting someone know you think they are special and you like them without having to actually say it. You don't have to go over the top, you just need to be that little bit more friendly than you are to everyone else. The four best tips on flirting are as follows:

Smile: The best way to catch someone's attention is to look them straight in the eye and smile. Try to do it as naturally as possible because there's nothing worse than a fake smile. And remember to do both things at the same time – or else he'll think you're giving him a dirty look. Often one smile will be all you need to get his attention.

Walk Over to Him: The next thing to do is to walk over to him. This is the hardest part and you may be tempted to get a friend involved here to be the mediator. My advice is DON'T! For a start, you run the risk of him thinking she's the one who fancies him. Secondly, it's embarrassing to have someone say,

"My friend fancies you". And worse, if you're shy and he's shy, your possible relationship isn't going to progress any further than this.

Say Something: Assuming that you follow the tip above, the next thing to do is to speak to him. Say something, say *anything* – just don't stay silent. You don't have to be massively funny or serious, just say "Hi!" and smile again. If he's not shy, hopefully he'll take the initiative and start a conversation with you. If he doesn't don't give up and try asking him a question. If you can, look at him when you speak. There's nothing more off-putting than having someone mumble something into your right shoulder that you can't even hear.

Listen: The one fatal mistake most people make when they are talking to someone they fancy is that they don't listen. Often we are so worried about how we're appearing to the other person that we're not even listening to what they are saying. If you don't listen, you won't know where to take the conversation and you run the risk of the person thinking you're just not interested in them.

WHO ASKS WHO OUT?

Good question this one. Old-fashioned people think it's the man's job to ask a woman out while some women think it's their job. The plain fact is, if you fancy someone and don't think they are going to take the initiative and ask you out, then there's nothing to stop you asking them.

There are no rules about who is supposed to ask who out. Boys aren't born with an ability to ask girls out. As I said before, they are just as afraid and scared of rejection as you.

Of course, it's hard to pluck up all your courage and say something, but believe me the first time you do it will always be the hardest. Once you see how easy it can be there will be no stopping you.

"The first time I asked a guy out I was scared. I thought he would laugh at me and all my friends would think I was some kind of desperate case. But it worked out okay. He was really sweet and not at all surprised and my friends thought I was brilliant."

Mia(15)

♡ Dealing with rejection

One of the hardest things about asking someone out is taking the risk that they might say no. This can seem like the most horrible thing in the world but you can cope with it in the following ways:

❋ At least you'll know that they are not right for you and you can go off and find someone who is.

❋ A person who doesn't risk anything doesn't get anything. If you're brave enough to risk asking someone out then you're 99% likely to end up with someone good.

✲ Just because someone turns you down doesn't mean you are bad or awful. It just means that you're not right for each other.

✲ Don't take rejection as a sign you are worthless. You are still the same person you were before you asked him out.

✲ Boys say no for a variety of reasons. Perhaps they don't want a girlfriend. Maybe they are heartbroken over someone else. Or they are just too scared to have a relationship.

♡ How to turn someone down politely

The other side of being rejected is having to say no to someone who has asked you out. Sometime, you may find yourself being asked out by someone you just don't fancy. If he's someone you or your friends make fun of, or someone you would never look at, it can be tempting to be nasty. DON'T. It takes a lot of courage to ask someone out and being vicious in your response can hurt someone really badly.

"The first time I asked this girl out, she turned round and laughed really loudly and said, 'Why would I date someone like you?'. I was so humiliated that I didn't ask another girl out for years."

Pete (17)

Always treat people the way you expect to be treated yourself. If you don't want to date them be nice. Make an excuse or just say "I'm sorry but I don't want to date anyone at the moment". You don't always have to be blunt and truthful. You should always respect anyone who asks you out, and be privileged that they took the time to do it.

♡ How to cope when you do/say the wrong thing

Saying no when you mean yes: How many times have you waited for the man of your dreams to ask you out, only to blow the whole thing by giving him the wrong answer? Saying no, when you mean yes, is more common than you think. Sometimes, it happens because we're so shocked that we've been asked out that the wrong word just pops out. Other times it can occur out of fear. Fear that your fantasy is now real. Fear that it will all go horribly wrong and fear that he's playing some kind of horrible joke on you.

However, unlike other fumbled beginnings, it's something you have to put right as soon as possible. This is because rejection stings and makes us feel bad about ourselves, and if the person who has asked you out feels rejected for too long, he won't want to go out with you at all. If you've given someone the wrong answer don't be afraid to be honest and admit you've made a mistake. Put it down to nervousness or stress and tell him that you do want to go out with him. This might mean swallowing your pride and asking him out but it's worth it if you like someone enough.

Ignoring them:
The strange thing about being attracted to someone is that it can turn you into a completely different person. I used to have this odd habit of being perfectly friendly, nice and witty to everyone except the person I fancied. I did it partly because I thought it was cool not to show someone I liked them and partly because I was afraid of what they would do if I did show them I liked them. I eventually stopped behaving this way when a boy I had once fancied asked me why I used to be so horrible to him. I was so horrified that I decided there and then I would never do it again.

Sometimes, it helps to look at things from another person's point of view to see what effect your behaviour has on them. Imagine if someone you fancied always ignored you or turned away when you spoke to them. Would you take it as a sign that they fancied you? Probably not! You'd take it as a sign that they were unfriendly and the last thing on your mind would be to go out with them.

If you like someone show them before they get the wrong message.

Laugh every time they talk to you:
Lots of people laugh when they are embarrassed. It's a way of coping and not having to say anything when your mind goes blank. But it's also a good way to offend someone who has plucked up all their courage to come and talk to you. If you laugh wildly everytime someone you fancy comes near, you risk appearing a fool!

There are two ways to control laughter. One way is to try and control your breath. This means breathing steadily when someone you like comes near you so you'll be less likely to giggle. The other way is to keep in mind a few questions that will get you out of anything. Something like:

"Are you having a good time?"
"Have you seen..."

If all else fails, be honest. Admit that you always laugh when you feel nervous as this will usually get them on your side. All people want to know is that you're not laughing at them. As long as people know this, you won't make them feel bad about themselves.

Doing something embarrassing: What's the most embarrassing thing you've ever done? I once ran out of a toilet with my skirt tucked into my knickers because I was in such a hurry to get the attention of someone I fancied. My friend once walked into a glass patio door because she was too embarrassed to wear her glasses in front of a boy she liked. Another friend ended up in hospital with a broken arm after she tried to impress a boy with her "skilled" roller blading technique.

As you can see most people have done at least one embarrassingly, cringe-worthy thing in their life. Though we all thought we wanted to die afterwards or at least spend the rest of our lives in our bedrooms, we *did* get over it. Embarrassing things happen to us all and if you laugh about it (even if you feel like crying) people will laugh with you.

The ability to laugh at yourself is the sign of a confident person and we all know how attractive confident people are.

In any case, if someone fancies you then doing something silly now and again isn't going to put them off you. If it does then maybe you should consider your choice of boyfriend. A person who takes themselves so seriously isn't worth fancying.

♥ Friends and love

When you're happy, there's nothing like letting your friends know what's going on. It helps you to re-live those happy moments over and over. Laugh at all the bad bits and maybe get some thoughts on what you should do next. However, there is a fine line between talking about what's going on to friends and letting them get involved. Say too much and you'll leave yourself open to gossip and jealousy. Two things that can kill a relationship even before it's got off the ground.

cringe!

My mate really fancies you!

"I fancy Mark's friend Tim. Mark is my best friend's boyfriend, so I've asked her to tell Mark to tell Tim I fancy him."

Sue (14)

Confusing? You bet! If you're tempted to let a friend ask someone out on your behalf consider this: It never helps your case to have someone else plead your side. This is because they are not you and will not say something the way you would have done. Perhaps they will ask the person out too abruptly or give the impression that it's all one big joke. Maybe they'll leave a bit of information out or even forget to say exactly what you actually asked them too.

Don't underestimate how scary being asked out can be. Most of us have an underlying fear that we might be the butt of some great joke, so to be asked out in a second-hand manner is frightening.

More often than not, you are tempted to say no, even if you mean yes.

Letting friends do all the work also takes the enjoyment out of the early stages of a relationship. Having a friend do all your running is rather like letting them experience a rollercoaster ride for you. You end up feeling cheated and left out, even if you asked them to do it in the first place.

Sometimes, we let friends do the asking for us because we're too afraid of being rejected. It's almost as if hearing the news second-hand will be less painful than hearing it face to face. Sadly it isn't. Not only do you end up wondering if some kind of misunderstanding has taken place but you also end up blaming your friend for being the bearer of bad news. The end result is, you'll end up falling out with your friend and not getting the boy you want. Save yourself the bother and do the asking yourself.

CHAPTER FOUR

THE FIRST DATE

It's tough going out with someone for the first time. You've probably got your parents breathing down your neck. (Who is he? Where did you meet him? Where are you going?) Your friends will be ringing up giving you "helpful" hints. And you'll be worrying about the actual date with the worst possible scenarios running through your head. It can also be hard to know if you're doing everything the right way and whether or not you are going too fast or too slow.

Whether we like it or not, we can't help but compare our relationships to those of others we know but this is something that hinders rather than helps us. No two relationships are the same and no two couples ever react the same way to love.

First dates are, perhaps, the biggest nightmare in the dating game because they are always loaded with anxieties about ourselves.

Don't be too late home now!

Isn't that dress a bit on the short side?

One bag of nerves

Will I be good enough? Will he ask me out again? Will he fancy me enough to kiss me? What if he hates me? And what if I do something stupid?

Then there's the added horror of being alone together. You may have dreamed about it for months but now it's about to happen fear rears its ugly head. Even though you know you're more than capable of holding an intelligent conversation, the thought of talking to HIM for a few hours is enough to have you shaking in your shoes.

What if there's a silence? What if you can't think of anything to say? Worse still, what if you can't stop talking? Should you let him take the lead or should you do it?

We all know how important it is to make a good first impression. An impression that will say, "I'm normal, bright, funny, pretty and together and that's why you should like me!". Not one that shows you to be a bumbling fool who drops food into her lap, can't get her words out and misses completely when she goes in for the kiss. If the latter brings back bad memories of dates you may have had in the past or think you'll have in the future, fear not. We all have dating disasters brought on by nervousness and stress and it's nothing to be ashamed about.

And what about the more physical aspects of dating? How are you supposed to kiss him if you've never kissed someone before? What should you expect when he does go to kiss you? Should you go for the kiss or leave it up to him? If you make the first move will he think you're pushy? If you don't will he think you're not interested?

Learning how to prepare for your dates is the first step in learning how to deal with your anxiety and fears. If you know where you're going then you can know what to expect. Better still, if you pick the place you'll feel even more comfortable and sure about what you do and don't want to do. As for the physical aspects, well, there's a way round those too.

Above all, don't be so hard on yourself. We all make mistakes when we're learning about love, in fact this is the best way to learn. When I first started dating I behaved in ways I would never behave now and, likewise, I'll say and do things now that I would never have done years ago. Love, boys and relationships are not things that fit like a glove into your life. It takes time to get used to having a boyfriend and time to work out what kind of relationship you want. It's only once you've sorted out those two things that you can finally work out what all the feelings you're experiencing mean.

❤ FIRST DATE TIPS

"Our first date was terrible. We went out for dinner and I was so embarrassed I couldn't speak so all I did was eat. Every time he asked me something I'd put some food in my mouth. It all went horribly wrong and I ended up nearly choking on a carrot."

Ellie (16)

"He asked me what I wanted to see and because I said I didn't mind he picked a really gory horror film. I spent the whole film practically gagging under my seat and afterwards felt so sick I had to go home."

Helen (17)

"I've been going out with Carl for two months but I thought I'd blown it after our first date. First I dropped buttered popcorn all over him, then I knocked his drink over and as I went to help him mop it up I accidentally head butted him. Later as we were leaving I let go of the door and it hit him hard, then I nearly poked his eye out with my umbrella in the rain. He said he thought he'd go home because he didn't want to risk having anything to eat."

Yvonne (15)

♡ Choosing where to go

Deciding where to go is one way of making sure you don't panic on a date. The cinema is always a very good option, because not only does it deal every nicely with the first two hours of your date but it also give you something to talk about when you come out. It will take your mind off worrying about what to say and do and is a good way of being close to someone without actually having to do anything. Make sure you pick the right kind of film for both of you. Comedies and thrillers are a safe bet, but soppy films or horror pictures aren't, unless you both agree you like them.

If neither of you have much money, think of things you can do for free. Like museums (they aren't all boring and dismal), parks, zoos or

do something active. Roller blading, swimming and tennis are all good ways to get to know each other. However, if your date does suggest going somewhere that you hate the sound of, don't just say no. Say, "Sorry, I'm not too good at swimming/ roller blading etc., but would you like to come to ...".

This way he'll know you're rejecting the idea and not him.

It also helps not to lie about what you do and don't know. Saying you are an Olympic swimmer when all you can do is the doggy paddle is bad news. Lies like this always get found out and you'll end up being humiliated on your date.

If the weather's terrible, you have no money and all else fails invite him round to your house to watch a video or play video games. This is best done when parents and younger siblings are not around! There's nothing worse than trying to get to know someone under the watchful and inquisitive eye of your entire family.

One last tip here. Don't put yourself through added hassle by agreeing to go somewhere where you'll know a lot of people. Friends, though helpful at times, can be off putting and irritating on a first date!

♡ Learning to talk to him

This is often the biggest worry on a date. After all, what can you do if the conversation dries up and you're left with a huge gaping silence? It's simple always have some stock questions and subjects in your head that are guaranteed conversation fillers.

Television/Films/Music/Books: Everyone has an opinion on at least one of these things. Talk about something you know a lot about whether it's a soap opera or your favourite band. This way you can talk until he gets up enough courage to say something. Even if he doesn't agree with you it will help you to get a good idea of what he likes and doesn't like.

Newspapers: It's always a good idea to read a newspaper or a magazine before you go on a date. They are filled with useless little stories that will never save your life but make good anecdotes when you're out. You can mention a story you heard about a man who was abducted by aliens or something like that. This way you'll lighten the conversation and hopefully get him talking.

Celebrity Gossip: People say they hate celebrity gossip but the truth is most people love to hear it. If you're an expert on it then go ahead and bring it up. However, try and be selective about what you say. Droning on about people he's never heard of or doesn't care about will only annoy him and make him think you're shallow. Give it five minutes and if he doesn't add anything give it up.

♡ Things not to fill in with

Gossip about people you know: This is always a dangerous one. Apart from the fact you may accidentally bitch about someone he knows and likes, it also doesn't sound very pleasant. He may also worry that you'll go behind his back and gossip about him and his friends.

Ex-boyfriends: A big no-no! No-one wants to hear about exs on a first date. If they were brilliant you'll make your present date feel insecure and if they weren't, why bring them up anyway?

Stories you've heard about him: It's tempting sometimes to say, "You'll never guess what someone told me

... And that Phil Bradshaw is a complete prat.

Phil's a good mate!

about you...". This is also dangerous ground. Apart from hurting his feelings (even if what you heard wasn't true) no one likes to think people talk about them behind their backs. Once he's heard the story you'll get into more of a mess because he'll ask who told you and when they said it.

It can sometimes feel hard to talk to someone you fancy because you imagine them to be this amazing person you've conjured up in your head. The reality is they are like you and me. They eat, drink, sleep, say silly things and do stupid things like you and me. They won't walk away if you say something foolish, they won't laugh if you mess up and they won't call you stupid if you don't know what they're talking about.

The trick of talking to boys is to imagine they are your best friend. Forget that you're faced with the man of your dreams and, instead, pretend he's someone you've known for years. Don't hang on to his every word and try not to avoid his gaze. This doesn't mean stare him in the eye all the time but try and be casual about things. It's tempting to laugh loudly when they say something funny – DON'T. You'll end up looking like a crazed maniac. Above all, don't despair if things go wrong. It's not the end of the world when a first date goes badly. Many people I know have had horrendous first dates with their boyfriends/girlfriends and have still ended up living happily ever after.

♡ **What to do when a date goes wrong**

First date hell happens to us all. It often occurs through a mixture of nervousness, shyness and clumsiness and isn't necessarily a sign that you are badly suited to someone. Of course, now and then, it can happen because you're dating the wrong person but this is pretty easy to spot right from the beginning.

If your date makes fun of you, takes himself too seriously, freaks out when you do something wrong and generally makes you feel like you are on trial, then you're going out with the wrong person.

"I went out with this guy who spoke about his ex throughout our whole date. I was nervous and my words got jumbled and he was really horrible about it. He said he liked women who could speak properly. Later I said how much I liked this band and he said his ex had much better taste than me. It was awful. The more I tried the worst it got."

Tina (15)

The best way to deal with a date that is going horribly wrong, is not to stick it out. What's the point of staying if someone is making you miserable or is being mean? You don't have to make a big show of it, just get up and say goodbye. Walking away is not only a dignified retreat but it also give a message loud and clear that you're not interested. On the other hand, if your date is going badly because you just don't fancy that person, then walking away in the middle of a date isn't your best option. Sometimes, we think we fancy someone only to discover on closer inspection that we don't. If this happens then be polite. Say you've had a very nice time but you just don't want a boyfriend right now. It's never nice to be rejected so always treat people with respect and never be nasty.

If your date's going badly because you've embarrassed yourself or there have been a few silences, don't worry. It's perfectly natural for first dates to be a bit wobbly. If you think you've made a big blunder, instead of feeling ashamed and humiliated, bring it up. Say "OOPS, sorry about that. I'm always doing things like that when I'm nervous/excited/anxious. I hope you don't mind". There's nothing worse than trying to pretend something didn't happen when it obviously did. Remember, he is as worried about making a good impression as you are. He doesn't expect you to be perfect in the same way that I hope you don't expect him to be perfect. So what if he fluffs a few lines or you say the

wrong thing, or a joke falls flat? These are things to work on and laugh about on a later date, not things to take to heart.

♥ KISSING

Kissing is a delicate subject for most people. We all worry whether we're any good at it and no matter how many times we've done it before we wonder whether this will be the time that we blow it. Sloppy kisses, fumbled kisses and fast kisses, they are all things we agonise over. Then there's the worry of who should make the first move and when to pull away. Lots of people even worry about breathing and noses that get in the way. For something that's meant to be so much fun it's certainly laden with all kinds of obstacles.

Well, let me start by saying there are no wrong ways to kiss, only wrong people. Kissing is something that occurs between two people who like each other. If it goes badly the first time then don't give up. There's no shame in saying "Whoops, let's try that again". As for breathing, well don't worry about that, breathe thorough your nose. While we're on the subject of noses, despite what you may think, they rarely bump unless you go in too fast and if they do just laugh about it and try again. Kissing is meant to be fun, not something so serious that it will ruin your life if it goes badly.

As for who goes first, well, that's up to you. If you feel comfortable go for it and if you don't, sit back and wait.

As for the actual technique, all I can say is learn to relax. Don't panic, don't worry, and don't imagine he's thinking the worst. Keep your mind on what you're doing and everything will be fine.

Please let my breath be fresh!

♡ French kissing

A quick note here about French Kissing. For those who aren't sure what this is, it's a form of kissing where both people open their mouths during the kiss and use their tongues to explore each other's mouths. If the thought of this makes you want to retch then don't do it. If you quite like the idea, and you trust your partner, then go for it. It can be a very intimate and enjoyable experience. Some boys aren't very well versed in kissing etiquette and may try to shove their tongues down your throats the first time your lips meet. Apart from being rather horrible it's also very annoying. If someone does this break away immediately and tell them to back off. Kissing, like any other kind of intimacy, should only be done if you feel happy and right about it. Never let anyone force you into doing something that makes you feel uncomfortable or worried.

CHAPTER FIVE

DATING PROBLEMS

So you've got a boyfriend, you've had that first date, and even survived the first kiss. What next? A carefree life of bliss and joy – well, if you're lucky, yes, but, if not, you're probably going to come across one of the following problems.

Everyone has heard the saying, "No man is an island", and in the same way no couple is an island. Your relationship may be wonderful when you're on your own but there's no way you can go around pretending nothing else exists. Friends, family, responsibilities and school all add pressure to a relationship, and sometimes even problems, whether you like it or not.

It's no good saying if it wasn't for exams, or his mum, or your best friend, things would be fine because you can't get out of dealing with the parts of life you don't like, even if you are in love. You may feel like you don't need anyone else in the world but the truth is you do. If you ditch your friends and family, where will you go if things go wrong?

If you give up your school work, what will you do to get a job?

If you ignore other people who love you, how will you feel when they eventually go off and forget about you?

Sure, love is the most important thing in the world, but not just the love you have for your boyfriend but the love you have for your friends, family, and yourself. So be sensible – don't neglect anything and anyone in your life just because you're smitten!

❤ PARENTS

Sometimes, it's hard to believe that your parents ever dated and went through the same feelings you're experiencing now. If they are still in love then they probably seem unsympathetic to all the worries you're going through. If they are single or recently divorced maybe they are bitter about love or no longer believe in it.

Whatever your situation, parents and dating hardly go hand in hand. For most girls, fathers can be a real obstacle. Not many want to see their "little girls" going out with a boy or hear you talk about love and relationships, never mind sex. As for mothers, you can be lucky and have an understanding one, or unlucky and have one who seems to always stand in your way and put down your boyfriends.

"Ever since I started dating I have had such problems with my parents. My father acts like he hates me and is always saying I'm going to get myself into trouble and that I'll end up pregnant at sixteen. My mum on the other hand always says mean things about my boyfriends, and makes out they are being unfaithful. I feel like they don't trust me or don't think I'm good enough to have a boyfriend."

Steph (15)

Parents always have motives behind their rules about boyfriends, sex and relationships. They are not doing things just to spoil your fun but because they are scared. Scared that you are growing up and away from them. Scared that you'll get hurt. Scared that you won't want to be with them any more. It's tough being a parent and knowing that you have to let your children make their own mistakes – and even tougher having to watch them make decisions you don't agree with.

It's also hard for most parents to accept that you are interested in sex, kissing and relationships. Most parents have selective memories and, while you may have had sexual feelings for years, they will still remember you as a cute kid with her hair in bunches, They don't want to know that you French kissed the boy next door or snogged someone in the school playground. They'd much rather you stayed a child so they didn't have to cope with your adult feelings.

If your parents say you can't go out with anyone, there are better ways to deal with it then flying off the handle and doing it behind their backs. Apart from proving all their worse fears, this will achieve very little. Start by looking at why they are being so strict. Have they come from strict backgrounds? Has the daughter of someone they know been hurt in a relationship? Have you given them some reason to be worried?

Knowing this will help when you talk to them about their rules. Point out that by being so strict, you feel they don't trust you or understand you. You may not get everything you want but you may be able to get them to compromise.

Remember, this is your chance to prove how mature and sensible you are, so go for it. Don't yell, stamp your feet or act petulant. Instead, tell them you want to go out with a boy because you really like him, and this doesn't mean having sex, getting pregnant or going steady. As long as they realise you are going to be sensible and not do something rash they will come round.

Ways to Keep Parents Happy While You're Dating

❋ Always come home from a date on time.
❋ Tell your parents where you are going.
❋ Introduce your boyfriend to them.
❋ Go out in a big group.
❋ Don't talk about your boyfriend all the time.
❋ Don't just have evening dates.
❋ Steer clear of love bites or any kind of marks that show you have been getting intimate with your boyfriend.
❋ Don't spend all your time on the phone talking to him or about him.

 FRIENDS

Blah, blah, Darren, blah, blah, blah, Darren. Darren, blah, blah, blah.

When you're in love, it's the most natural thing in the world to want to tell all your friends all about it. You want to share your happiness and let everyone know how wonderful your life is and that's great, but be careful. It's really easy to overdo things and before you know it your friends will be mad at you. Any good friend will want to hear about your relationship but they won't want to hear about it all of the time. There's nothing worse than having a friend who goes on and on about her relationship and forgets to ask about anyone or anything else.

If you are currently being swept off your feet by love, don't forget that everyone is not as happy as you and therefore, not everyone will be happy for you. Seeing a couple in love does strange things to some people, and before you know it you could invoke feelings of jealousy, rejection and competition from your friends. They may feel left out and turn spiteful or feel you're showing off and keep away from you. As for friends who are breaking up or unhappily single, have some consideration for their feelings and be careful not to go on about your love life and make them feel bad about themselves.

Another problem with telling friends everything about your love life, is you leave yourself open to gossip and misunderstandings. People like nothing better than to comment on someone else's private life and before you know it you could find yourself the subject of much unwanted speculation. People think if you tell them lots of personal things, they have the right to interfere and give unwanted advice. Save yourself the hassle and keep your private life private.

"Everyone knew about me and Gary because we were so pleased when we started going out we'd go around and tell everyone how in love we were. The next thing we knew we'd come into school and hear we'd broken up or that he was going off me. Or that I'd got off with someone else. It was all lies and we could never work out who was making them up. It put a really big strain on our relationship."

Georgia (16)

If you are going to talk about your relationship, be very careful about what you say and what you keep secret. Some things, especially the more intimate aspects of your relationship should always be kept between you and your boyfriend. Other things like worries and complaints should be kept to a few special friends who you can trust. If you're too vocal about what's wrong in your relationship, it will get back to your boyfriend and cause trouble.

♡ Boyfriends who don't get on with friends

One of the hardest problems I ever had was disliking my best friend's boyfriend. He was obnoxious, arrogant and selfish. He thought *I* was obnoxious, arrogant and selfish. My poor friend spent the whole time trying to stop us tearing each other apart. It was a strain on her, a strain on her relationship and a strain on her friendship with me. Luckily we worked it out. We agreed to be nice when we saw each other, which thankfully wasn't very often. The point I'm making is just because you love your best friend and you love your boyfriend, it doesn't necessarily mean they'll love each other.

If you're lucky they will, and all your problems will be solved but more often than not there'll be a fair share of jealousy and competition between them. They might both struggle to get your attention, criticise each other and basically get you to choose between them. If this is happening to you YOU DON'T HAVE TO CHOOSE.

It's up to you who you want to be friends with and who you want to date. Tell them if they care about you, they'll have to compromise and share you and that's all there is to it.

♡ How to lose your best friend

A guaranteed 100% way to lose your best friend is to ignore them every time you've got a boyfriend and run back to them every time you're single. And who can blame someone for dumping you if you do this? No one likes to feel like they are being used. Friends are not there to keep you busy until you find love. They are an important part of life and if you lose them you'll always regret it. It's perfectly easy to have friends and a boyfriend, but it's not easy to just have a boyfriend and no one else. You need your friends no matter how in love you are, so don't neglect them.

♡ SCHOOL AND RESPONSIBILITIES

The first stages of love are quite unlike anything you'll ever experience and this is why it's known as the honeymoon period. You may find yourself on a constant high where all you need and want is each other. Everything else will feel unimportant and a waste of time. After all, it can be hard to concentrate on anything, let alone all the things you usually hate, like school, homework, and part time jobs. You may feel what's the point to doing this and that when all you want is to wander around in a daze of love?

Yet, realising that normal everyday life goes on is important, and even though you may feel everything has paled into insignificance next to your relationship, it hasn't.

We all have responsibilities that have to be faced no matter what and though everyone is pleased you're happy they are not going to be pleased if you start dropping out of things and forgetting to do the things you've promised to do. Friends won't thank you for letting them down, parents will get on your back if you all you do is talk about love and your teachers won't be happy if you neglect your school work.

Love and life can easily go hand in hand, you don't have to choose one over the other. All it takes is a bit of management. This means organising yourself. Taking time to make sure you're not forgetting things and setting time aside for your relationship and day dreams. There's plenty of time for everything, as long as you remember that your relationship is only part of your life and who you are.

♡ Rows

So you've started to fight all the time and you don't know why? Sometimes people bicker about silly things when they haven't got the courage to bring up the real things that are bothering them. Is this you? Do you pick on your boyfriend for the way his hair looks because you're furious about something else? Does your boyfriend moan at you for being late because he's mad you talked to your ex?

If you are the person on the receiving end of someone's complaints it can be hard to see what the real problem is, especially if you're sure you're not doing anything wrong. If you feel you're being picked on, then speak up. Ask what's really wrong and try to get to the bottom of the problem before the bickering tears you apart. If you're the person who's always complaining then make a decision to say what's really on your mind, rather than just complain. Boyfriends aren't psychic – they can't read what's on your mind and what's upsetting you. They don't know that you hate it when they do this or say that and the only way they are going to stop is if you say something.

After all, the key to making sure rows don't ruin your relationship is communication which means talking and listening. When faced with criticism, most of us go on the defensive and immediately stop listening. Our hackles rise and we take everything a person says to heart. We become so worried about being wronged that we forget to hear what's being said and the problem never gets solved. So, if you want to communicate learn be honest and really hear what your boyfriend is saying, even if it's hard to take.

By the way, talking doesn't mean shouting, swearing, crying, or walking away when you hear something you don't like. It means being able to take constructive criticism and work on it. If you're the person doling out the woes make sure you don't overdo it and make sure all your criticisms are constructive.

You'll always be able to tell if your rows signal the end of your relationship or not. If you argue constantly and go home unhappy every night, then maybe it's time to call it a day. If your rows are always about faithfulness, sex, flirting, and other serious topics, it may also be a sign that you aren't right for each other. But if you fight now and then, it's not the end of the world. Very few relationships get by without disagreements of some sort. Even if you never argued in the beginning and do now, it doesn't mean your relationship is terrible. Most couples in the honeymoon period (the first stages of love) live in a state of bliss. Then reality sets in, their love calms down and becomes something deeper. This is when a balance between real life and love has to be found and that's what some rows are all about.

Is THIS LOVE? HOW TO TELL

It can be tempting to say "I love you" long before you actually mean it. It's one of those phrases that's bandied about with such regularity that you feel you should say it, whether or not you actually want to. It's hard to know when you're in love and even harder when there's so much pressure from everyone to announce it.

Before you actually say it, you should work out what it means to you. For a start, are you saying it for the right reasons? If one of the following is true for you, then maybe you're not.

Your boyfriend says it: When someone says "I love you", it's hard to not say it back. But if you don't mean it, don't say it. People don't always fall in love at the same point and maybe he's more sure of you than you are of him. Or maybe love means something completely different to him. Don't feel pressurised to say it until you're sure.

You've been going out for two weeks/months/years: There is no time limit to when you should or shouldn't feel love. Some couples go out for years without ever feeling it, whilst others take only a couple of days. There are no "shoulds" to love. Only say it if you want to.

You think it will make him stay: There are some people who use love as a form of emotional black mail. They think if they say it enough times and loudly enough, it will make their boyfriend or girlfriend stay with them. The sad fact is it doesn't. Saying "I love you" is no guarantee of anything. It's just a way of expressing your emotions and feelings. It doesn't mean you have to have sex or stay forever or even be more caring. It's just something you say when you feel deep affection, passion, admiration, and trust for another person.

♥ WHAT LOVE ISN'T

Nearly everyone I know, including myself, has been in at least one relationship they thought was true love, and that clearly wasn't. At the time friends, family and even people we hardly knew tried to get us to see the truth but we all refused to. The fact is, sometimes, relationships go horribly wrong and yet, still we stay. We stay because we hope things will get better. We stay because we feel guilty or scared. We even stay because we don't want to be single or don't want to believe things have gone so badly wrong. And other times, we stay simply because we don't realise that what were experiencing isn't love but something else all together.

♡ Abusive boyfriends

Boys who hit their girlfriend, for whatever reason (and there never is a valid one), are trouble and need serious professional help. Statistics show women who are battered by their boyfriends get hit approximately sixty times before they leave. It's easy to blame yourself and say, "It's my fault" or "I started it". And it's just as easy to say, "He's always so sorry" and "He's promised never to do it again". The fact is, he will do it again and again and again, until he gets help. Don't be fooled into thinking you can change him or help him, the best way to help him is to help yourself and this means leaving before he hurts you.

♡ Abusive girlfriends

Are you an abusive girlfriend? Do you attack your boyfriend or scratch, kick and punch him? If you are, you're not alone. There are hundreds of girls who do these things to their boyfriends. It comes from anger, frustration, and despair and, like abusive boyfriends, you need to get professional help. You can't blame your boyfriend for goading you into it and you

can't excuse it by saying, "But I still love him". Help yourself
and seek advice from a trained counsellor.

♡ Smothering

Smothering someone in supposed love just to make sure
they don't stray isn't about love, it's about control. Love isn't
keeping such a tight hold on your boyfriend that he can't say
or do anything without your permission. Likewise love isn't
having a boyfriend who says you can't go out with your
friends, wear make up or sexy clothes. If you love someone
you should trust them and, if you trust them, you shouldn't
need to smother them.

♡ Addictions

Having a boyfriend with an addiction to drink, drugs, glue
sniffing, or gambling is a tough one. You may feel responsible
for him, or too guilty to leave, or feel that you can change him.
But these feelings have little to do with love.

Until someone with an addiction admits they have a problem,
and wants to get better, they will never overcome it. This
means no amount of loving, crying, or pleading is going to do
them, or you, any good. Likewise, ignoring their problem will
just make it easier for them to be an addict. You have to
realise that their problem is *their* problem and not *yours*.
However, it is essential that you protect yourself from the
effects of their addiction and this, more often than not, means
walking away and seeking outside help for them. Call Adfam
on 0171 638 3700 for advice.

CHAPTER SIX

SEX

"How can I tell when the time is right to have sex? I have been going out with my boyfriend for a month and I'm still not sure."

Julie (15)

"My boyfriend is pressurising me to have sex with him. He says if I really loved him I would."

Jackie (15)

"I've had sex with four boys and I haven't loved any of them. It hasn't really made any difference to me. But my friends say I am awful. They say if I don't love them I shouldn't be having sex with them."

Anne (17)

If you really loved me you'd have sex with me.

Sex and love, love and sex. For some people they are the same thing, for others they are a world apart. One of the greatest myths of our time is that sex equals love and vice versa. It's more than possible to love someone and not want to have sex with them. And it is more than possible to have sex with someone and not be in love with them.

Never let anyone fool you into thinking that having sex will prove the value of your love. If you love each other, you won't need any proof like this. Likewise, having sex because you hope it will make someone fall in love with you is a road to heartbreak and disaster. It will ruin your self-esteem, your self-confidence and your faith in yourself. Love is something that takes time and only happens when you know, respect and admire someone. Of course, it is possible to have enjoyable sex without love, but sex can be a million times better when love is involved.

♡ VIRGINITY

Virginity is a hot topic of debate. For many people it is still a sign of pureness and of being a "nice" girl. This is basically a load of rubbish. All virginity means is that you haven't yet had sexual intercourse. It isn't something to boast about in the same way that having sex isn't something to shout about. It doesn't make you a better or worse person. Virginity, like sex, is a personal thing and no one else's business but your own. If you don't believe in sex before marriage then that's okay. If you do, well that's okay too. If you don't want to have sex and you're well over the age of consent then that's also your choice.

I'll warn you now, there are plenty of people out there ready to make you feel bad about being a virgin. They'll tease you, call you names and basically try their utmost to get you to have sex. If someone picks on you for this reason then you need to look at why they are doing it. If it's a friend maybe it's because they regret losing their virginity or know it's something that will hit a nerve with you. If it's a boy, he maybe doing it because he wants his way or his friends are making him feel that it's uncool not to have sex.

"My boyfriend used to go on and on about sex until I turned round and said 'If that's all you want, get lost'. Then he admitted he didn't want it at all but his friends told him he was wet for not trying it on with me."

Laura (15)

Whether you are a virgin or not, the important fact to remember is, you always have the right to say no. Whatever your age and whatever your past. It doesn't matter if you've let your boyfriend touch your breasts, kiss you a hundred times and buy you dinner. You still don't have to do it. It also doesn't matter if you've had sex with your last boyfriend or the one before. If you don't want to do it this time, then you don't have to. Even if you said you would have sex and now you've changed your mind. *You can still back out.* Having said this, it's also important not to lead boys on if you have no intention of having sex. Make your position clear from the beginning, say how far you're willing to go and then you won't have to worry about misunderstandings.

Of course, if you've decided that the time is right and you want to have sex, it's important to always be sure of your reasons. If any of the following are true for you then you may be about to make a big mistake.

- You've heard sex is a wonderful experience.

✱ All your friends are doing it.

✱ He says he'll leave you if you don't.

✱ You feel too old to be a virgin.

✱ It will make you feel more mature.

✱ It will give you something to talk about with your friends.

✱ It will make a boy like you.

✱ It will prove you are attractive.

✱ You want some experience.

✱ It will stop you feeling left out.

Remember, having sex is a simple thing to do but living with it the day after isn't. If you haven't protected yourself, or have gone through with it for the wrong reasons, you're going to regret it.

So, you're sure you're ready

If you really think you and your boyfriend are ready for sex then make sure you do it the responsible way. This doesn't mean drink loads of alcohol because you're nervous, use the withdrawal method (*not* a form of contraception) and hope for the best. It means talk about contraception and don't cheat on each other. Sleeping around carries a huge risk. The more lovers you have, the more likely you are to contract a sexually transmitted disease and pass it on.

If the first time you have sex together is a disaster then don't despair. The first time is rarely like the movies. The earth doesn't move, fireworks don't go off and it doesn't go on for hours. Perhaps, it will all be a bit embarrassing, maybe it will hurt, or you'll get upset with each other. If this happens, you've probably had an experience similar to hundreds of other people. Sex is like any other activity, it takes time to get the hang of it and time to find out what you and your partner likes. Even if your boyfriend has had sex before, it won't necessarily make him a great lover. Try not to let bad sex experiences drag you down. Good sex happens when two people feel physically, emotionally, and spiritually close to each other. This comes with good communication and affection for each other.

Feeling ready for sex is also about more than using a condom and being faithful. It's also having regular check ups to make sure you're healthy. This includes cervical smears, and internal examinations. A horrible thought, I know, but the only way a doctor can make sure you're healthy inside.

If you ever think you may be pregnant or have a sexually transmitted disease seek help immediately at your GP, Brook Advisory Centre or Family Planning Clinic. Missing a period, getting a strange discharge, pain, and itching are all signs that something may be wrong.

Above, all remember that sex is like any other activity – you should never do anything that makes you feel uncomfortable or hurts. People like all kinds of different things and, if you're not experienced, you can be tricked into thinking something is a normal part of sex when it may not be for you. This is why it can often help to talk to someone before you start having sex. Brook Advisory Centres (telephone 0171 713 9000 for details of your nearest clinic) have trained counsellors who will answer any question you may have on sex and sexual relationships.

♡ Age of consent

The age of consent for girls is 16 years old. This means "by law" it is illegal for any male to have sex with a girl who is under 16-years-old. Contrary to popular belief, this doesn't mean you have to lose your virginity the minute you hit sixteen or that you're a "slut" if you lost it before. This age is a legal device used to protect young girls from abuse. Age, in fact, has little to do with having sex.

"I lost my virginity when I was thirteen, it was awful and I always regretted it. I thought it was so bad because I was young. Then when I was seventeen my best friend told me she had just lost hers and she regretted it too. Now I think bad experiences have more to do with who you are having sex with and why, than the actual act."

Donna (17)

If a girl under 16 does have sex and is found out, it's the boy and not the girl who can be prosecuted. If you are both the same age it is unlikely your boyfriend will be prosecuted. But if your boyfriend happens to be a lot older than you, he could be arrested and receive a prison sentence.

♡ Contraception

Making a decision about having sex also includes making a decision to be safe and use contraception. The 1985 House of Lords' ruling in the Gillick case changed the law on contraception in the UK. It now states that doctors have the right to judge whether or not they think a girl is mature enough to receive contraception. A doctor will judge this on a girl's ability to understand the choices s/he is offering her and her reasons behind wanting contraception.

Many young people steer clear of their doctors and health clinics, thinking if a doctor says no, s/he will also tell their parents. The fact is, even if your doctor considers you to be too immature s/he has to keep your visit confidential. This means s/he cannot tell your parents.

If you are at all worried about visiting your family GP, you can visit a Brook Advisory Centre (telephone 0171 713 9000 for details of your nearest clinic) instead. They specialise in giving free and confidential help to young people on contraception and sex.

♡ Getting contraception and advice

Though it is against the law for a boy to have sex with a girl under 16, it is not illegal for anyone to use or buy condoms even if they are under 16. Condoms are available from all kinds of shops, chemists, supermarkets, and even petrol stations. You can also get them free at any Family Planning Clinics or Brook Advisory Clinics.

♡ HOW TO SAY NO TO SEX AND STILL KEEP YOUR BOYFRIEND

One of the main reasons people lose their virginity is because they don't know how to say no and still keep their boyfriend or girlfriend. Sex is such an emotive subject that rejection can easily seem like the end of a relationship. But it doesn't have to be this way. Being honest about why you're saying no will help to keep your relationship healthy.

The very first thing to do it make it clear you're rejecting sex and not your boyfriend. We are all very self-conscious about the way we look and how we feel about our bodies. Sometimes, a no can be taken as a sign that you don't fancy a person and this can lead to all kinds of misunderstandings. When you say no, talk about why you don't feel ready to have sex. This means being honest about how you feel, what effect his pressure has on you, and why you want to wait.

Next, really listen to what your boyfriend says. Boys are under a tremendous amount of pressure to have sex. They are made to feel it's something that all boys do and if they are not doing it, or can't persuade a girl to do it, then they are a failure. Feeling a failure not only makes them lose self-

I won't go to bed with you but I will go to the cinema.

confidence, but it also makes them act badly. If you have said no to your boyfriend and he is freaking out, then ask him why. Getting to the bottom of his desperation to have sex will take the pressure off both of you and hopefully solve some of your problems.

It's also important at this time to make it clear that just because you have said no right now, doesn't mean that you will always feel this way. As you get older and your relationship grows, the chances are you will change your mind. In the meantime, what's all the rush? If a boy isn't willing to wait until you are ready, then he's not the right boy for you.

❤ **A TROUBLESHOOTER'S GUIDE TO SEX**

Worries about sex include more than worries about the law, virginity and contraception. Often, more emotional and social questions pop up, like "If I sleep with him will I get a name for myself?" or "Am I normal not to want a lot of sex?". Below I run through some common sexual dilemmas and show you how to stick to your guns when everyone's telling you what to do.

♡ **Does sex equal being a slut?**

Anyone who calls a girl any of the following needs their head examined: "slut", "slag" or "easy". They are all stupid things to say. The fact is some girls sleep with a lot of boys, some girls don't. Some boys sleep with a lot of girls, some boys don't. Sadly, double standards still persist and, while it's considered macho for a man to have had loads of partners, it isn't seen as being the same for women. People who judge others on this basis don't deserve any kind of attention from you. Whatever you do it's your choice and yours alone. Girls can be as sexually active as boys, no matter what people say.

However, if you are someone who has sex with a lot of people and then always regrets it, you may need to question why you do it. It doesn't mean you're abnormal but it could mean you have a low self-esteem and are hoping that sex will improve it. Sadly, I don't need to tell you, it won't.

♡ Your boyfriend is demanding sex

The only way round a problem like this is to never give in to a boy's demands over sex. It doesn't matter how many times you've had sex before or if you are a virgin, if you don't want to have sex then don't do it. Some boys think if you're no longer a virgin then you're up for sex all the time. This isn't true and it's up to you to make it clear that past experiences have nothing to do with the present. Some girls find they have sex once and then they don't want to have it again. If this is the case then that's also okay. Sleeping with your boyfriend isn't an agreement that you will do it every day from now on. No one has a right to dictate what you should and shouldn't do with your body.

If a boy is pressurising you to have sex, then he doesn't have your best interests at heart and this is a sure sign that he's wrong for you. Some boys may try to fool you with lines like:

"It's unhealthy to be a virgin."

"It's bad for me not to have sex when I have an erection."

"This is all your fault. If you weren't so attractive I wouldn't be asking for sex."

"All my other girlfriends have done it."

If they try any of these lines on you, show them the door.

It's all your fault.

Having sex to keep a boy interested, or to prove you are attractive won't give you the results you want.

♡ Am I frigid?

"**F**rigid", "ice-box", "cold" – these are just some of the names thrown at girls who choose not to have sex. They are totally meaningless names and the only way some boys deal with the fact their girlfriends won't have sex with them. It's sexual pressure and there are no other words for it. Frigidity doesn't exist. It's just a made-up term that boys use as an excuse when a girl says no.

Some boys are extremely competitive with their friends and not having sex can seem like a failure in their eyes. This is why they can turn nasty when you turn them down. If this is the case with your boyfriend, don't let it sway you. If he only wants sex so he can boast about it with his friends, then who needs that?

Sometimes, you may wonder if there is something wrong with you for not wanting sex. If you do, let me put your mind at rest. Tensing up and feeling panic when a boy tries to have sex with you happens because you are not ready. It doesn't mean you are cold or there is something wrong with you. Likewise, having bad sex with someone isn't a sign that you're rubbish at it. Bad sex happens when you have the wrong partner or are doing it for the wrong reasons.

♡ How often should you have sex?

There are lots of statistics about how often people have sex, but they are just statistics and nothing else. When it comes to sex there is only one "should" – YOU SHOULD ONLY HAVE SEX WHEN YOU WANT TO AND AT NO OTHER TIME.

Sadly, some people feel that once they have sex there is no going back to holding hands and that they can't turn round and tell their boyfriend they no longer want to do it. The fact is if you are having sex with someone you should be able to communicate with them. If you can't talk to them then why are you having sex? There are a lot of boys who would be mortified to discover that you were only having sex to please them. If you love someone then be honest and talk to them about it. As long as you make it clear you are not rejecting them, only sex, they won't be hurt.

♡ Peer pressure

It's not only boys who have friends that are competitive about sex. Female friends can be just as bad. We all know someone who goes on and on about sex. About how great it is and about how many times she's done it and what you're missing out on. However, her boasts don't actually mean she honestly loves it, they mean she's not sure she's doing the right things and, by shouting about it, she's trying to convince herself.

Some friends will tell you they have had sex loads of times and that you are the only one left who is a virgin. Again, this is peer pressure and you can deal with it simply by saying "So What?". Even if you did happen to be the last virgin on earth (which is extremely unlikely), what difference would it make?

Real friends would never try to push you into something just so you could belong. Remember this and don't let any one force you to do something you'll later regret.

CHAPTER SEVEN

THE SEVEN DEADLY SINS OF LOVE

There are many ways to make a relationship work and even more ways to make one fail. No one's saying you have to be a perfect girlfriend who smiles all the time and never feels jealous when her boyfriend's eyes stray. But, at the same time, if you go crazy every time he looks up, then you're asking for trouble.

Part of any relationship is learning to cope and control the nastier sides of your personality. The sides that aren't always pleasant and rational. The sides that are jealous, insecure and frightened.

"My first boyfriend left me for my best friend and since then I've kept every boy I've dated away from my friends. It's

not that I don't trust my boyfriends it's more that I don't trust myself to stay calm. I know I'd spend the whole time imagining something was up, even if it wasn't."

Anna (15)

"I am a naturally jealous person. I go crazy when I see someone flirting with my boyfriend and I get even worse if I think he's flirting back. I know I behave badly and that my boyfriend hates the way I behave but I can't help it."

Susan (16)

It's more than natural within any relationship to have moments when you feel jealous, possessive, or wronged. However, if you constantly feel one or more of these emotions, and act upon them, your relationship is heading for trouble.

From your point of view it isn't great to feel such anxiety about your relationship the whole time. It will make you irritable, unhappy and depressed. Love is supposed to be fun and easy, not something that robs you of your self-confidence and makes you feel bad about yourself. From your boyfriend's point of view, no one likes to feel suffocated, spied on, or mistrusted. If you are constantly pushing your boyfriend, or accusing him of things he hasn't done, you will eventually push him away.

Remember, trust is a huge part of love. If you don't trust someone, then you don't respect them, and if you don't respect them how can you love them?

JEALOUSY

Jealousy is that great, green-eyed monster that rears its ugly head when you least expect it, and makes you behave like some crazed person for very little reason. If your boyfriend really does flirt with other girls, two-times you or is completely untrustworthy then you have good reason to be jealous. You also have good reason to stop going out with him and find someone who really does deserve you.

green-eyed monster

DIARY

If your boyfriend is always pleading his innocence and complaining you're jealous for no reason, then it may be time to take note of what's really going on. Jealousy is born out of doubts about our own self-worth. When we don't feel good enough for someone, we can't believe anyone else will think we're good enough. Therefore, we spend the whole time thinking some "better" female is going to some along and whisk the person we love away.

"I spend the whole time being jealous because I think my boyfriend wants a prettier, and nicer, girlfriend than me. When we go out and I see him smile at another girl, I panic and think I'm losing him. That's when I get jealous and cling on to him and make him miserable."

Mona (16)

Sometime, jealousy swamps a person so much that they can't see how irrational they are being. If you're not sure about whether or not you are a jealous person ask yourself the following:

- 💜 Do you hate it when he smiles at other women?
- 💜 Do you take note of the females he talks to and laughs with?
- 💜 Do you go mad when he mentions his exs?

💜 Do you keep your female friends away from him?

💜 Do you complain when he chooses to spend time with his mates rather than you?

💜 Do you wonder about his female friends?

💜 Do you read his diary to find out what he's been doing?

If you answered yes to one or more of the above, your jealousy may be out of control.

The best way to deal with jealousy is to look at the reasons why you're giving in to it. If you've been hurt in the past it's easy to see why you feel jealous, but until you learn to trust you won't ever have a relationship that works out. Likewise, making demands on your boyfriend to always behave a certain way for your sake is unfair. If he's naturally sociable, you can't ban him from talking to other girls. If he's good looking, it's not his fault other girls look at him, and if he's funny, people can't help being drawn to him.

Think of all the reasons you like him and you'll see why others are drawn to him too. It's also important to understand that, just because the two of you are in love, it doesn't mean that neither of you will ever find someone else attractive again. It's a fallacy that you stop noticing attractive people when you're in love. You stop wanting and fancying them but you don't stop seeing them. In the same way that you may look at a handsome guy that walks past you so will your boyfriend look at attractive women. There's nothing wrong with this and it's perfectly natural.

If you feel your jealousy is getting the better of you, don't try to hide it. Talk to your boyfriend and tell him how you feel. Explain why you feel jealous and listen to his reassurances. At the same time make a real effort not to check up on him, don't suspect the worst all the time, keep away from his diary and don't interrogate him every time he comes round late.

♥ MANIPULATION

Are you guilty of manipulation? Do you cry to get your way? Do you sulk if your boyfriend says no to you? Do you use sex as a weapon? Do you flirt to get back at him? If you do any of these things then you're being manipulative.

Manipulation is basically a way of controlling a situation to your advantage. It's a way of setting up something and then getting a person to play right into your hands. For instance, crying, or sulking when you don't get your way, in the hope your boyfriend will give in to you.

The fact is manipulation works, but only up to a point. If you cry when you're upset, that's fine but if you cry all the time, then there's going to come a point when your boyfriend won't take you seriously any more. And who can blame him? Crying because he's hurt your feelings is fine, but crying because he won't watch the video you want...? Well, that's ridiculous! You

are in control of what you say and do, and you crying constantly or sulking is something you can stop. It's just a habit and like any habit you can break it.

If you are being manipulative it's worth looking at the reasons why. Is it because you don't like feeling vulnerable? If it is, then don't worry. Love makes you feel vulnerable because you've opened up and trusted someone.

Vulnerability is okay. It won't break you but manipulation may break your relationship.

If you're being manipulative because you like being in control then you have to realise that you can't control someone's feelings and emotions. Love has to be given by a person not taken and if you start to push someone around they won't stick around for much longer.

Sometimes people become manipulative out of boredom. Are you twisting situations because you're bored in your relationship? Are you trying to find something to hold on to and some point to your relationship? If you are it may be time to call it a day.

♥ PLAYING GAMES

Some girls like to play games in relationships. Games that attempt to get their boyfriends to prove their love. Games that attempt to show their boyfriends that they are worth more than they may think. These little tests of love rarely have anything to do with love. More often than not they are just an ego boost and a way of making yourself feel more secure at someone else's expense.

Are you someone who makes your boyfriend jealous on purpose, or leads him to believe that lots of people are attracted to you? I have one friend who once played this very game with her boyfriend. Every time they were out, she'd point out guys who had flirted with her and make it clear that they still did when he wasn't around. One day she went too far and told her boyfriend she had once kissed one of them, even though she hadn't. Her ploy was to see how jealous she could make him in order to see how much he cared. Sadly, her plan backfired and he dumped her because he felt betrayed. If she had only listened to him, she would have seen that he really did love her.

Playing games like this is dangerous because you always run the risk of losing. It's also a nasty thing to do because if you love someone you shouldn't try to make them feel insecure and jealous just for your own gratification. Don't beat about the bush, if you want to know how your boyfriend feels, ask him. If you want to know why he's behaving badly, ask him. If you've heard he's been flirting with someone, don't try to get back at him, first find out if it's true.

If you feel your boyfriend is playing games with you, then tell him to stop. No one likes to feel like a pawn in a game of chess. Love is about more than this.

♥ HIGH EXPECTATIONS

We all have extremely high expectations about love and what it can bring us. If you watch any movie about love, you can be fooled into thinking love can transform a mundane existence into something wonderful. The fact is, being in love can make you feel better about yourself and your life but it isn't the answer to all your problems because this initial feeling doesn't last forever.

In the same way, expecting fireworks, stars and constant joy isn't what love is about. There will be days when you feel all these things and more but there will also be days when you feel bored, annoyed and fed up with your boyfriend. That's the way love is, a delicate balance between good and bad.

Also, beware of making your love life one big soap opera.

BOYFRIENDS AREN'T PERFECT- ONLY HUMAN.

Intrigue, secrets, and hysterical outbursts make good TV but not good relationships. Sometimes, it can be tempting to be over dramatic about a relationship, in order to make it more exciting than it actually is. If you are bored and fed up, then creating dramas is just delaying the inevitable. If you feel bored then break up and find someone new. Don't make things harder for yourself.

Having high expectations about what love should and shouldn't feel like is also painful in the long run. Boyfriends aren't perfect, only human. They can be insensitive, say the wrong things, and be embarrassing. Imagining them to be something superhuman will only lead to disappointment on all sides. They can't solve everything that's wrong in your life and it's wrong to think they can. Love is different for different people and just because your best friend never tires of her boyfriend's company doesn't mean you will feel the same way about your boyfriend. An old school friend of mine used to always worry that her boyfriend and her weren't really in love because they didn't want to see each other all the time, like her sister and her boyfriend. Then one day her sister asked, "How do you do it? I'm always so jealous of your relationship. It's so exciting compared to mine. All we ever do is sit in together and watch TV".

As much as we judge the value of other people's relationships, it's impossible to know what really goes on behind closed doors. We may think someone has an idyllic love life full of kisses and great sex but the reality may be very different.

"Everyone always said what a great couple we were. What a laugh that was. The minute we were alone all we'd do was fight and call each other names. He didn't trust me and I never trusted him – some great love affair that was."

Annie (17)

It's also important to remember that passion isn't about having huge rows, being jealous, fighting and then kissing and making up. Passion is about having strong emotions for someone and caring about them.

Expectations are fine but don't let them rule your life. There's nothing definite about how and what you're supposed to feel. Give yourself time to feel all the things you want. So what if you don't feel passionate about your boyfriend? In time you could change your mind. It's the same with love. You may feel you'll never love anyone the way the people in the movies do, but when you find the right person you'll find the right kind of love.

❤ TWO-TIMING / TELLING LIES

Lots of people think they can get away with being unfaithful if it's just one stolen kiss or a quick one night stand. But which ever way you look at it, two-timing is two-timing and there's no way round it. If you desperately feel the need to be with someone else, then at least do the decent thing and end your relationship first. Some people like to play around because it makes them feel more attractive and needed. Others like to do it while they have a girlfriend/boyfriend because then they get the best of both worlds. Then there are the people who do it to test the water. They are too scared to risk being single so they like to make sure they have someone waiting in the wings before they end one relationship

Two-timing is a horrible thing to do to someone. It makes them feel used, second-best and bad about themselves. It destroys their self-confidence and leaves them wondering "Why?". Don't treat someone this badly, do the right thing if you want someone else.

If you have been two-timed, and your boyfriend wants to come back, then it's up to you to decide what to do. Some people do make silly mistakes and it's only by losing what they've got that they realise what they want. If you do decide to take them back, make sure you can forgive them. It's no good taking them back only to constantly make them feel bad about the past. Forgive and forget – or don't take them back at all.

♡ POSSESSIVENESS

So you love him and all you want is to be with him all the time? You don't want him to spend time with his friends? You don't want him to play football and you don't want to share him when you go out? Unless you want to lose him, you'd better learn to shape up.

No two people can exist alone without anyone else, and just as he needs his friends and other interests, so do you. It's boring having to spend all your time with one person and it adds unnecessary pressure to a relationship. Sure it's nice that you want to spend all your time with him and lovely that you feel so good about him that you don't want to be without him. However, he was a separate person before you met him and he still is, even if he's now your boyfriend.

Possessiveness is a bit like being slowly suffocated. Your boyfriend may love you more than anything in the whole world but if you are constantly making him choose between you and other things, he isn't going to thank you. Give him space and you won't be sorry. If you start making him feel guilty every time he goes off he's not going to want to see you at all.

Remember, boyfriends are just a part of your life, and should never be your whole life. Don't fall into the trap of giving up everything for him. If you do you'll be sorry and very lonely when he leaves you. So next time he goes out, don't sit in waiting for him to return. What about your friends? What about your interests? You aren't just someone's girlfriend, you are an individual person, with a life of her own.

♥ INSECURITY

Nothing can kill a relationship quicker than insecurity. When we're insecure we tend to over analyse everything that is said and done, thinking, "He said that, so he must mean this, so I have to respond in this way". Don't think for him, if you're worried about something, get it out into the open and don't just assume you know what he's thinking because you'll always assume the worse.

It's also natural in any relationship to feel worried about his past and his exs but if all you do is ponder on it then you are going to drive yourself and him into the ground. Remember, his ex is his ex and you are now his girlfriend. Bringing the past into the present will do nothing but cause problems. Everyone is entitled to have a past and whether they regret it or not is up to them.

Just because your boyfriend was a pig to his last girlfriend doesn't mean he will be one to you. He deserves a chance as much as the next. Try not to compare yourself to his ex-girlfriends, you don't have to be like them, or live up to them. You are your own person and that's all that matters.

If you feel constantly insecure you need to ask yourself if it's justified. Does your boyfriend give you reason to be insecure? If so, why? And why are you putting up with it?

Some people feel insecure until they hear the words they want. If you feel insecure because you are desperately waiting for your boyfriend to declare his love and he hasn't, don't take it as a sign he doesn't care. In my opinion "I love you" is an over-rated term. People say it far too easily and there's a lot to be said for someone who waits until he is sure. In any case, "I love you" isn't some kind of promise. It doesn't mean "I'll always love you" or "I'll stay with you forever" and it isn't a solution to feeling insecure.

CHAPTER EIGHT

BREAKING UP

When you start a relationship the last thing your want to do is think about splitting up. If you're very lucky maybe you won't. There are couples who fall in love and never break up, but the great majority of us aren't that lucky. We have to go through numerous relationships and break ups before we find the right person.

Falling in love is no guarantee that your relationship will last forever. People and situations change and this means relationships change too. Perhaps everything was wonderful when you were at school, but now you're thinking of going to college and he's got a job, suddenly things aren't so easy between you. You no longer have the same aims and this means you can no longer spend all your time together. Maybe your relationship has changed for more personal reasons. Divorce, bereavement, and illnesses all cause people to make major changes in their lives and relationships. Sometimes, people just fall out of love with each other. There doesn't have to be some great reason, it's a just a feeling that things aren't right and need to change.

Yet, change isn't a bad thing. We all have to change in order to grow or else we become stale and boring. Maybe you don't want to change and can't see why he wants to. If this is true then perhaps you are no longer right for each other.

Break ups are painful for all kinds of reasons. Firstly, there's the rejection to cope with and that horrible feeling that comes when someone you love doesn't want to be with you any more. Then there's the element of failure that takes over. Failure because you didn't make it work. Failure because you couldn't make him stay. This inevitably leads to loss of confidence and a feeling that you are somehow to blame. Then there are friends and family to tell – the list of things to do and feel just goes on and on.

Sometimes we can see a break up coming a mile off and know it's for the best, and yet we cling on for dear life. It's rather like being on a sinking ship. You hang on because you're too scared to let go. Worrying that you might drown if you fall into the water, completely forgetting that you will drown if you stay on board.

Letting go and diving into the water is the only way to survive. Break ups are sad and hard, but you can, and will, survive them. I'm not going to lie and say they don't hurt, because they do. Yet, once you come through them, I can guarantee that you will be a stronger person, ready to give love another try.

♡ TIME TO BREAK UP

Breaking up is hard to do, whatever side you are on. If you are on the receiving end, it's painful and scary. If you're on the giving end, it's painful and scary. No one breaks up with someone for fun. It's a tough decision and even harder when you know the other person loves and relies on you.

Having been on both sides, I can honestly say neither side is easy. In fact, being the person who makes the break can sometimes be harder. For a start, you get a lot less sympathy and support. Next, you spend a lot of time feeling guilty and wondering if you've made the right decision. Whereas, if you are the person who's been dumped, you have no choice but to cry and get on with things. If you feel your relationship is going nowhere, and you need to end it, do it! Don't be one of these people who tries to be nice and ends up making things worse. Sometimes you have to be the bad guy and there's no way round it. Be truthful about your feelings, and don't lie to try to make the break up easier for someone. The truth is you can't.

P.S. I don't want to go out with you anymore.

"I didn't know how to tell Steve I no longer wanted to date him so, before I went on holiday, I told all his friends, hoping they'd tell him. I suppose I thought it would be easier on him if I didn't tell him face to face. Of course, it was only easier for me. He was so hurt. He said I had humiliated him in front of everyone and hasn't spoken to me since."

Karen (16)

"I stayed with Johnny because I couldn't bear to hurt him. I used to say I loved him and wanted to be with him just because I didn't want him to feel bad. I even used to hate kissing him. Then one day we had a fight, and I just blurted out that I didn't love him and never had. It was awful, he went really quiet and then cried. Later he told everyone I was a bitch and had lied to him from the beginning. It was so awful but, in a way, he was right."

Helen (17)

Staying in a relationship for someone else's benefit is a waste of time. They won't thank you for it and neither will anyone else. Sometimes, we tell ourselves we're staying for the other person's benefit when the truth is we're doing it for ourselves. We don't want to be the bad guy because we don't want to feel guilty. Or we don't want to be single.

"I know I don't love Tom but he cares about me and looks after me. It's not selfish because he gets what he wants and I get what I want. I know he thinks I love him but what good would it do either of us for me to tell him the truth?"

Marcia (16)

If you don't love someone, sooner or later the truth will come out. It's unfair and selfish to wait until someone else comes along and makes your decision easier. Some girls try to goad their boyfriends into doing it because they are too scared to do it themselves. This is shirking your responsibility. If you don't want to be with someone, then be honest and have the decency to tell them. Anyone who enters into a relationship is taking the risk that it may not work out. Remember, no matter how much you love someone, no one wants a girlfriend or boyfriend who stays out of pity.

❤ IF YOU'RE ON THE RECEIVING END

Being rejected by someone you love is a terrible thing. When you love someone you tend to believe everything they say and do is right. Therefore, when they ditch you it can be easy to take this as a sign you are worthless or not good enough. It's horrible being in love with someone who no longer loves you back and even worse when they are nasty about it.

Whatever they say, don't analyse it to death. Sometimes, break ups are inexplicable and no amount of dissecting will ever get you closer to the truth. If they were horrible, take it as a sign that you are well rid of them. You are better off without someone who is nasty enough to hurt you any more than is necessary. Above all, remember you are still the same person you always were. The same person they once fell in love with. All that has changed is their perception of you and what they want. Thinking you can become what they want to make them stay is dangerous, and will only make you more unhappy.

FIGHTS, ARGUMENTS AND TEARS – WHEN TO LET GO

Remember the good old days when you messed about, laughed a lot, and generally had a good time? What happened to them? Now all you do is fight, bicker, and pick on each other. Perhaps those habits of his you once loved, now annoy and irritate you? Maybe your taste in music gets on his nerves? Or you yell at each other instead of talk, scream instead of listen?

Often, people fight like this when they are too scared to say what's really on their mind. Fighting is a sign that something is wrong within a relationship. Couples who love each other don't pick on each other all the time. They don't make each other feel bad and score points every time they get their way. This isn't love, this is a battle ground.

Of course, some couples like to fight. It's a part of their communication and, as long as they are both happy with it and thrive on it, then that's fine. But if it's driving you into the ground then it's time to change things. If you're fighting and can't stop, then it's time to talk. When I say talk, I mean talk and listen. Hear what your boyfriend is saying and why. Often, when a couple are mad at each other, they are so worried about being misunderstood that they forget to hear what's being said and the arguments go on. The only way you're going to change a relationship that's going wrong is to talk. However, be warned. Sometimes, all the talk in the world will get you nowhere. If you don't know what you really want or why you are unhappy, perhaps, it's time to step away from the relationship for a while.

If you step away and still can't fix it then, as the old saying goes, "It's no good crying over spilt milk".

If you spend more time being unhappy than happy within a relationship, then it's time to leave. If you spend most of your time crying, or being miserable, then it's time to get out. If you yell so much that you're always exhausted and unhappy – then what are doing with this person?

♡ HOW AND WHY DID IT HAPPEN?

If you have just been ditched you're probably wondering WHY? Why did this happen? Why did he leave? Why didn't I see it coming? All I can say is break ups happen for lots of different reasons, some good, some not so good. Sadly, not everyone is trustworthy and not everyone is honest about who they really are. People disguise themselves and pretend to be things they are not. You may be unlucky enough to end up with someone who doesn't deserve you and will treat you badly. Maybe they will two-time you or leave you for your best friend? Or perhaps they will lie to you and leave you feeling bewildered and foolish.

"When I met Rob, I thought he was the nicest boy ever. We went out for three months and I was so happy the whole time. Then one day he told me he had been having an affair

with my friend for two months. I was so crushed that I blamed myself. I kept thinking, how could I have trusted him? How could I have believed him? Why was I so stupid? Then I found out he two-timed all his girlfriends and I suddenly realised he was the one to blame not me."

Carly (16)

Being ditched for someone else isn't easy to handle. Apart from all the obvious feelings of rejection and hurt you're also left feeling ashamed and humiliated. No one likes to feel they are in competition with someone else, and suddenly finding that you are is horrible. I once fell in love with an extremely accomplished liar. He spent half his time telling me how much he loved me and the other half sleeping with other girls. I finally realised I was onto a real loser when I accused him of two-timing me with a girl we knew. He said, "I'm not yet, but I'm thinking about it". I was hurt, I was sad, and then I got angry. People who treat people like this, don't know the meaning of love. Don't put up with a boy who two-times you. It's a waste of energy and it says more about the kind of person they are than the kind of person you are.

Likewise, if someone dumps you publicly, gets a friend to do it for them, or just starts dating someone else and hopes you'll understand, don't bother trying to get them back. Boys like this are too immature to date and don't deserve your attention.

❤ EXPLANATIONS AND MESSY ENDINGS

"I wish I just knew why he finished with me. I keep thinking maybe it was because I said that, or did this. If only I knew."
Tina (16)

Sometimes, you'll have to put up with a messy ending where there are no explanations. This is difficult because, when you're hurt, you'll want to know why it happened and whether or not you were to blame. Sadly, if the person who has dumped you won't give you an explanation, there's not a lot you can do. By all means write him a letter, call him and try to get him to open up, but if he won't then give up.

People sometimes behave badly and don't know why they do it. Maybe it's something in their pasts or something personal that they don't want to talk about. It could be that they are afraid of commitment and intimacy, and yet don't know how to express it.

Running around trying to clean up the ending and make it all nice and rosy won't work. It won't make you feel better, and it won't make everything all right again. We can often get hung up on endings, trying to make sense of them, because this is a way of avoiding our grief. We think, if only we could find the answer to this everything else would be okay and easier to cope with. The fact is, this isn't true. Even knowing exactly why someone left you doesn't make heartbreak any easier to deal with.

Don't, whatever you do, make the mistake of begging someone to come back. When someone says it's over, 99% of

the time they mean it. Pleading and crying will get you
nowhere, whereas holding up your head (even if it's painful)
will help you to at least respect yourself.

♡ LEARNING FROM MISTAKES

One of the best things (and there are a few good things)
about breaking up with someone is assessing your
relationship. This means having a close look at what you put
up with, what you enjoyed, and what you hated about it. It's
only by looking at a relationship this way, that you can make
sure that you don't repeat old mistakes, and get the best out of
your next relationship.

There's a lot to be said for
not letting history repeat
itself. If you keep going out
with guys who two-time
you, ask yourself why? Is it
because you start dating
them when they have
another girlfriend? If it is,
then the chances of him
two-timing you in return
are quite high. Boys who
two-time do so because
they have low self-
esteems, and always need
to be reassured that they
are attractive. If someone
has a girlfriend and says
they fancy you, then make

sure they fancy you enough to finish the relationship they are in first, before you get involved.

If you keep dating guys who are selfish, arrogant and flirt with all your friends, ask yourself why? Sometimes seeing what initially attracted you to them will give you the answer. Was it his sociability? His biceps? His looks and charm?

If was something physical, or external, the chances are you overlooked the most important quality – his personality!

With hindsight, there are a lot of things we do in relationships that we would never do again. Things like putting up with someone who is always late and someone who lets you down at the last moment. Or someone who pressurises you into sex. Try not to feel bad about these things, it's only by doing them that we learn that we'll never do them again. That's what mistakes are all about.

♥ BOYFRIENDS WHO WON'T ACCEPT IT'S OVER

Sometimes you are going to find yourself in a situation where your boyfriend won't accept you want to break up. This is when you'll find that not everyone takes being ditched in a dignified way.

Maybe he'll start ringing you up and sending you letters. Letters that plead for you to come back. Or perhaps he'll cry, and make you feel guilty, hoping you'll relent. It's awkward, scary, and annoying when someone you once loved starts to behave in this way. Most people feel bad enough over a break up without having to be faced with constant guilt staring them in the face.

If this is happening to you, you may be tempted to try and make life easier for them. Maintaining contact, meeting up and talking round in circles for hours may feel like you're being understanding but it is not helpful in the long run. People who have been ditched will look for signs that you secretly care. Anything you say, or do, can be misconstrued and taken as evidence that you will one day return. I'm not saying you have to ignore them totally, only you have to be very careful about how you handle them. Every time you do something make it clear that your relationship is over and you only want to be friends.

Some exs may try to blackmail you into staying with them. Some very disturbed ones may even threaten to kill themselves if you leave them. Don't be tempted into giving in to this kind of emotional blackmail. If a boyfriend threatens suicide because you're leaving, then tell your parents right away and get them to contact his parents. He is not your responsibility and you don't have to stay tied to him out of guilt and worry.

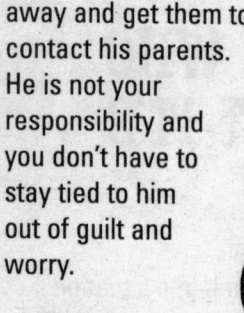

CHAPTER NINE

SURVIVING THE HEARTBREAK

It's all over. He's left and now you're on your own. But are things really over? If you're like 99% of the population they're not! The chances are, you're feeling so upset you can't get on with your everyday life. Perhaps, you cry all the time, or walk around in a permanent daze. Or maybe you don't really believe he's gone for good, and you're waiting for him to come back. It's likely that you also have moments where you feel depressed, and then other moments when you feel manic with happiness. Don't worry, these aren't signs that you are going mad, they are common symptoms of heartbreak.

Heartbreak is our natural response to the loss of someone we love. It has no time limit and no two people suffer it in quite the same way. You may find that your friend got over her ex-boyfriend in two weeks, while you're still suffering the early stages after two months. Or you could find that someone else's heartbreak lifts after only a few days. Either way, it doesn't mean you're pathetic or your love wasn't real. It just means that you need a different amount of time to come to terms with what has happened. Don't fool yourself into thinking you can skip being heartbroken. The only way to conquer it is to grieve.

Of course, after a break up, it's easy to walk around pretending you don't care. Yet putting on a brave face proves nothing. People expect you to be heartbroken, and no one will think less of you if you admit how much you're hurting. We all know how distressing it is to lose a person you love. It makes you question everything about yourself, what you believe in, what you want, and who you are.

Grief itself is a puzzling process. I'll tell you now, that it can knock you for six, make you wonder if you're going mad, and take considerable effort to get through. Hearing this may make you think you don't want to go through it and maybe you'll try to avoid it at all costs. However, as anyone who has gone through heartbreak will tell you, it's a process that always makes you stronger in the end. It will help you to realise that you can overcome someone leaving you and this in turn will give you the courage to fall in love again.

♡ HEARTBREAK – THE FOUR STAGES

♡ Shock and denial

Having someone say "I don't love you any more" or "I don't want to go out with you" is one of the most horrible things you'll ever have to hear. It will probably make you feel sick to your stomach, it may make you cry, or it may render you completely silent. There's really no graceful way to take being ditched. Some people go crazy, others just shrug it off. But underneath we all feel the same despair of rejection. The same "Why me? What have I done to deserve this?". This will be swiftly followed by shock and denial that will leave you feeling completely numb and empty.

Why me?

"After he said it, I just went home and stared out of my window. I couldn't read, I couldn't listen to the radio, I couldn't speak. All I could think was I wanted to die."

Frances (16)

"When he dumped me, I felt so weird. It was like he was talking to someone else and I wasn't really there. It felt like I had imagined it all. Even the next day I couldn't remember if I had dreamt it or if it had really happened."

Susan (16)

In the early days of a break up, your life may feel completely unreal. People will expect you to respond in all kinds of ways. They may want you to rant and rave and be angry and cry. If you don't do any of these things, they may start to wonder why or ask you if you're really heartbroken at all. Don't, whatever you do, fall into the trap of putting on a show for others, or imagine there's something wrong with you.

You will cry and shout when you feel ready and, in any case, tears aren't the only way to express pain and hurt. Don't despair about feeling so cut off. Shock and denial does have its value. Explanations about break ups are painful and people can be very insensitive. Being in shock can help to protect you when you have to go through the early days of telling people what has happened and why.

♡ Depression

The next stage of heartbreak is depression. Once the truth sinks in, you're likely to start feeling bad. Maybe you'll lie in bed all day or stop going to school. Perhaps, you won't want to face your friends and imagine that life is worthless on your own. Or perhaps you've stopped eating, or have started eating all the time.

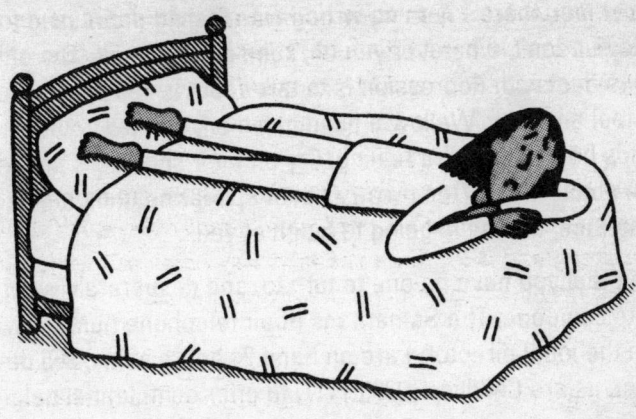

"At first I just couldn't get up in the morning. I felt tired all the time and then I would have a terrible headache all day. I also lost my appetite and started to get ill all the time. Finally my mum took me to the doctor and he said I was depressed and arranged for me to see a counsellor. Seeing her really helped because for the first time I started to understand what was happening to me and why."

Wendy (16)

Depression is a natural response to feeling rejected, afraid and alone. If this is the first time you have broken up with someone then it's likely the hurt you're experiencing is also frightening you. You may be thinking "What's the point of loving someone if all it brings is this pain?" Or maybe you've decided that you're never going to fall in love or trust someone again.

If it's not your first break up, you may be blaming yourself and wondering why this keeps happening to you. There is no real answer to this apart from saying sometimes we get unlucky and have a couple of bad boyfriends in a row. It isn't your fault, and reproaching yourself will get you nowhere.

Remember, there's nothing wrong with feeling depressed for a while but don't, whatever you do, keep it to yourself. The only way to deal with depression is to talk about it. Tell people how you feel and why. Wallow a bit, moan a bit, and tell your friends how bad you're feeling. Cry on their shoulders and let them comfort you. Don't worry about appearing undignified or losing face, no one is going to laugh at you.

If you feel you have no one to turn to, and desperately want to talk to someone, The Samaritans (their telephone number will be in the local directory) are on hand 24 hours a day, 365 days a year, as are Childline (0800 1111) to offer confidential help.

♡ Anger

Just when you think you'll never stop feeling sad and miserable, something else happens – you get angry. The funny thing about anger is, it literally happens without thinking about it. One minute you're feeling bad and blaming yourself for the break up. The next, you're aiming everything outwards. Don't worry about this stage, it's perfectly natural. Think of yourself as having been in hibernation and now waking up. The first thing you want to do is blame someone for all that time you spent feeling bad and hiding away. The obvious choice is your ex! If he's smart, he'll keep his distance. If not, you could end up having a few shouting matches.

"It shocked everyone, especially me, when I finally got angry. Up until then I had been blaming myself for my boyfriend's two-timing. Then, one day, I just stopped feeling sorry for myself and that was it. The next time I saw him I let rip and terrified the life out of him. He never came near me again."

Maria (17)

The one thing to watch out for with anger is the desire for revenge. Maybe you want to get back at him and you'll do it by dating one of his friends or telling people his most private secrets. Tempting as this is, *don't do it*. It won't achieve anything and will just make you feel bad in the long run. It will also help to get you a pretty nasty reputation. Revenge is never sweet, no matter how badly someone treated you.

Use your anger in a positive way because this will give you the strength to get your life going again. It will help you to realise that you do have a life without him and, what's more, it will probably be a better one. Forget about revenge and "showing him". Get on with making a success of your life without him.

♡ Acceptance

The final stage of heartbreak is accepting that everything is really over. This can also be quite a sad stage and make you feel quite nostalgic for the past. For the first time you may start remembering a few of the good times you had, instead of all the bad things. It's also a time when you'll consider that perhaps, your boyfriend was right about your break up, and that you weren't really all that happy together.

Don't worry about the fact you still think about him. Breaking up, and accepting it, doesn't mean forgetting the past completely. There will be times when you still think about him and that's okay. We all have fond memories of ex-boyfriends and happy times. We all talk about the past because it's what has made us the people we are today. Don't take it as a sign that you're still wallowing in pity, because you're not.

It's hard to imagine a time when you won't think about him at all but it will come. I sometimes look back at old photos and I can hardly recognise boys who once meant so much to me. Whether you believe it or not, he won't always be the last thing you think of at night and the first thing you think of in the morning. He won't always make you rage with fury, and the thought of him won't always make you cry.

FRIENDS AND FAMILY

One of the best things about breaking up with boyfriends is you discover the people who really care and love you. The people who will always be there for you, and won't trample all over your feelings. The ones who'll love you when you're horrible and when you're nice. These are the people who you should turn to for support and love – your friends and family.

In the early days, it can be hard to trust anyone. You may feel that everyone is secretly laughing at you or saying "I told you so". Maybe they are being too nice and too comforting. Or, perhaps, they keep telling you how you're well rid of him and that he was a pig any way.

All these things can be hard to deal with, but don't turn away, because you can't get through heartbreak without your friends.

People try to be nice in all kinds of ways, and sometimes they get it wrong. This is why it's up to you to tell them what you do and what you don't do. Not many of us want to hear that the boy we're crying over is a loser because it makes us feel like a loser too. But well-meaning people don't realise this, and you need to point it out.

Likewise, some people will try to get you to "snap out of it". Again, you have to tell them you need time, not bullying, to get over what has happened. It's also easy to take out what has happened on family and friends. But getting angry and mad at them will achieve very little. It will make you feel more alone and upset. Talk about how you feel. Explain what you think went wrong and listen to what people have to say. You won't always go on and on about what happened. One day, you'll just get bored of it, and then you'll stop analysing it for good. Give friends and family a chance to help you, because this is the one way you'll discover that you haven't changed and this in turn will help you to stop blaming yourself.

 TIME - THE IMPORTANT FACTOR

There are two common phrases that are guaranteed to make you mad after a break up. One is "There are plenty more fish in the sea", and the other, "In time you'll get over it". The former phrase is very irritating because you don't want another fish, you want the one you lost, and anyone who can't see that is a fool. The latter, as annoying as it is, is actually true.

Time is an amazing healer and just because you feel distraught, sad and bitter now, it doesn't mean that you'll feel this way tomorrow, the day after, next week or even next year. Grief has a funny way of changing overnight. You think you will feel heartbroken for the rest of your life and then one day you wake up and it's gone. Sure you'll have moments when it returns but it will never be as overwhelming as it was in the beginning. Likewise, thinking nothing compares to your ex-boyfriend, and, therefore, your life is empty without him, is also something that will pass. In time you really won't always be so mad at him and you may even find that you can become friends of a sort.

REBOUND

Some people deal with heartbreak by jumping immediately into a new relationship. They think if they fall in love again they can forget the fact that they are unhappy, depressed and scared. Sadly, this doesn't work. If you do this, it will only make you more insecure in your next relationship. Refusing to acknowledge your feelings doesn't make them go away and sooner or later they will emerge.

Of course, the other important factor to consider when you rush into rebound is your new boyfriend's feelings. Are you really dating him because you like him? Or are you trying to prove to everyone, especially your ex, that you don't care about the break up? Using people isn't the answer to your heartbreak.

It can be hurtful when you see an ex-boyfriend immerse himself into a new relationship. It can feel like he didn't really love you and that he is trying to make a point. However, this isn't always the case. Lots of boys, especially ones that are immature, can't deal with being on their own and would rather grab another girlfriend immediately than look at why their relationships go wrong.

❤ HEARTBREAK THAT LASTS

Sometimes, a considerable amount of time will pass and you will still find yourself feeling hurt and bitter about a break up. If you don't feel you've ever got past the moment you broke up, then you have to look at why. If you can't get over your heartbreak, it could be because you would rather hold on to your pain than admit to yourself that your relationship is really over.

Occasionally, people choose to stay unhappy because it makes them feel as if they are still involved with their ex. Letting go of the unhappiness means admitting things are really over. It can be scary to do this, especially if you have lived with your heartbreak for a long time. Lots of people define themselves through their feelings and, if everyone has got to know you as this person who is very hurt all the time, it can be difficult to change. However, real friends and family want you to be happy and will want you to move on.

❤ STAYING FRIENDS WITH EXS

This is a tough one. When you first break up with someone it's tempting to try and remain friends with them. Lots of people think "We had so much together, it would be stupid to throw everything away". While I agree with this, I also believe that friendships with exs only happen after time has passed. Pretending to be friends straightway is too hard because the chances are, you're only doing it in the hope he'll wise up and come back.

You'll probably find yourself doing the same things you always did for him but feeling angry when you do them. You could also find yourself feeling bad every time he goes out without you. Or jealous every time he talks about another girl. If you were really just friends, you wouldn't feel bad about these things and you wouldn't mind that he had a life without you. The one telling question that will determine your motive is this: "If your ex got a new girlfriend tomorrow could you still remain friends with him?".

If you could then, you are on the way to being friends. If not, then you're sticking around for the wrong reasons.

Being friends with an ex can only happen after you've worked out all the anger and frustration that came with your break up. Being just friends is fine but can you really deal with the loss of intimacy and closeness? You can, if you keep some distance between you, but not if you keep running to him when things go wrong. Going from lovers to friends is a huge adjustment. Take the time and space to make sure you do it properly.

CHAPTER TEN

BEING SINGLE

There comes a time, after all the recriminations are over, all the tears have been shed and all the shouting finished when you realise this is it – I'm single again. When you discover this you will probably feel a mixture of emotions ranging from excitement to sadness and back again. Excitement, because you can get back out there and do whatever you like, after weeks or months of feeling depressed. Sadness, because you know you're going to have to deal with people who are going to make you feel bad about being single.

Young, free and definitely single!

We all know that being single isn't as easy as it should be. If you don't have friends trying to set you up, there's your mum asking why you're still single, or your relatives wondering what's wrong with you. It's almost as if being single is something to be ashamed or humiliated about. Sadly, double standards still persist and it's still much easier for a boy to be single than a girl. This is because girls who are single are often seen as being threatening. Some people will never see your single status as something you are happy with because they could never imagine being happy on their own. They'll imagine you to be so desperate that you'll stoop to anything to steal their boyfriend! Other people see boyfriends as status symbols and therefore think anyone who hasn't got one is losing out. We all know this is rubbish but that's how double standards persist.

You might hate the thought of being single and that's why you held on to a relationship long after it was over. But being single doesn't have to mean nights in front of the TV with your cat and a big box of chocolates for company. Any social activity you do with a boyfriend, you can do on your own or with friends. Of course, it's hard when the whole world seems to be in love but the plain fact is all of us will be single at some point in our lives.

Being single has lots of advantages. For a start look at how many of your friends are downright miserable and fed up in their relationships. What do they complain about? Being trapped? Being bored? Feeling insecure and unloved? The list is probably endless. Next, change your perspective on life. Instead of thinking how alone you are, think of all the things you can choose to do on your own. Think of all the boys you can flirt with, all the future relationships you're going to have and how you'll never have to fight with your ex again. Then think of your friends and family, they are there and still a huge part of your life and so you're not as alone as you think you are.

♥ THE GOOD, THE BAD AND THE UGLY

Do you feel a failure because you're single? If you do, you're not alone. The hardest part of a broken relationship is dealing with the failure. The failure that you didn't make it work, the failure that he left you and the failure that you're now single. The trouble with break ups are they are so public. There's no way you can hide away and pretend nothing has happened, because everyone knows the truth. Yet, if you look at it another way, broken relationships aren't a failure. What's so bad about saying "This isn't working" and moving on? What's so bad about admitting you don't fancy anyone and that's why you're on your own? What's so terrible about doing what you want, when you want without having to consult anyone else? Nothing, of course, and that's what being single's all about.

Boyfriends and love are wonderful when they are right for you and terrible if they're not. Don't throw yourself into any old relationship just to prove something to other people. Anyone foolish enough to pity you for being on your own doesn't deserve your time or attention. There's nothing pitiable about being single, but there is something tragic about a girl who dates boys just to prove something to her friends and family.

Of course, it's never easy to stand your ground when people are pressurising you to date but the next time someone throws a "Why are you single?" or "Why don't you go out with so and so...?" or even a "Don't you want a boyfriend?" at you, use one of the following replies:

"I said I was single, not desperate."

"I haven't met anyone I like enough to date."

"I do have a life without a boyfriend."

"Mind your own business."

People like nothing better than to get involved with other people's personal lives. Don't encourage others to speculate about your life by whinging on about being single or talking about wanting a boyfriend. There's nothing wrong in wanting one, but complaining about it all the time won't get you anywhere.

Prove to others that you are fine by getting on with your life. Do the things you want to do now, and don't wait until you have a boyfriend to do it with.

The fact is, no one ever found a boyfriend or a life by just sitting about doing nothing. Boys like girls who are confident, adventurous, and have a mind of their own. They want to date someone who likes them for themselves, not someone who just wants a boyfriend as a status symbol.

Of course, the other thing to consider when you're single is whether you want a boyfriend at all. It's a popular misconception that everyone who is single wants to go out with someone. There are plenty of people quite happy to be on their own. People who like the fact they aren't serious about anyone and can do what they want, when they want. If you've had your fill of relationships for the moment then that's fine. Don't feel bad about it. It doesn't mean you'll feel this way forever, or you'll end up being single all your life.

When the time is right and you meet someone you like, you'll start going out with someone again.

COPING WITH LONELINESS

"I keep trying to be positive about my break up and get on with being single but I just feel so lonely all the time. I can't help wishing I had a boyfriend."

Melissa (16)

Battling against loneliness is the hardest thing when you're single. There will be times when you think, "I wish I had a boyfriend to cuddle", or "I wish I had someone to go to the cinema with". However, we all know that boyfriends aren't the answer to loneliness. Plenty of people are in relationships and still feel terribly lonely.

Studies on loneliness show it occurs as a direct result of lack of human contact and communication. If you feel lonely it could be because you've cut yourself off from everyone. It's difficult to go from a close and intimate relationship to being on your own. You will naturally miss the warmth and comfort that comes with it and yearn for something to take it's place. In a recent study, 25% of people admitted to feeling lonely at least once a day and 70% more than once a week. And half of these people were in relationships.

It's also important not to confuse being alone with being lonely. Solitude is not the same as loneliness and, just because you're on your own, it doesn't mean you are completely alone. You are still the person you were before you started dating. The person who has friends, a family and a life far away from being someone's girlfriend. The way to conquer these feelings is to talk about it with your friends and family. Admit how you feel and get them to help out when these feelings strike.

Then start by making a new social life for yourself. This can mean recreating your role within a group of people. If people have always known you as Mr. X's girlfriend then it's about time you asserted your own identity. This means showing them what you're your own person with your own ideas and beliefs. This can be a really liberating experience if you try it. It's also important to remember to make an effort. Don't always think you're being a burden to others – you aren't their charity case, you're a friend in need. Remember, if you don't call anyone they'll assume you're busy and will do things without you and you'll be left feeling on your own.

Often after a break up you will also need to prove to friends that you're a real friend, not someone who just comes round to use up all their Kleenex and talk at them till their eyes glaze over. If you want to show them there's more to you than having a boyfriend, start by not talking about you all the time. Be interested in what they do and what's going on in their lives and learn to laugh about the past.

Laughter is, after all, a great cure for unhappiness. Hurtful past experiences can be turned into amusing anecdotes, to will help you to see the lighter side of a break up. For instance, I remember an ex-boyfriend who used to insist on doing handstands when we walked down the street! After remembering this, I started to wonder why I even missed him. Another friend recalls a very fit ex-boyfriend who made her feel as if she wasn't good enough for him. Then one day she remembered how he used to sing Barry Manilow songs while he pumped iron – and suddenly she didn't feel so bad any more.

♥ DATING – SHOULD YOU OR SHOULDN'T YOU

Of course, there will come a time when you do want to date again. It happens when you're sure you're over the past and no longer think about it all the time. If you do, good for you! Love, despite all the bad stuff, can be a pretty nice experience. What else can make your skin tingle, your heart flutter and your knees go weak? What other kind of relationship can put you on a high in one second flat? What else can you rely on to give you that look or that smile?

The first step in dating again is to make sure you're doing it for the right reasons. Ask yourself this – Why do you want a boyfriend? Is it because you're lonely, fed up and miserable? I hope not. Hopefully, it's because you've met someone nice or someone's asked you out, or even because you just feel blissfully happy and want to share it.

If you've met someone you really like, then the dating game starts all over again but this time you'll have a better idea about what you're doing. Remember the following and you won't go wrong.

✳ Don't forget all the things you've learnt by diving into the deep end. Saying yes to a date or asking someone out isn't necessarily saying yes to love and a lifelong relationship. You may want to date but you may not want a serious relationship straightaway. If this is the case then be clear about your intentions and don't lead people on.

✳ Don't keep dredging up the past. One mistake we all make is to tar a new boyfriend with an old boyfriend's brush. Just because your last boyfriend was a lying, cheating swine, doesn't mean your next one will be too. Trust him, and don't always imagine the worst.

✳ Sometimes, when we haven't dated for a while and have been hurt, we can build up a fantasy figure of the kind of man we now want. That's fine while it remains a fantasy but trying to make a someone fit this image won't work. You can't always protect yourself from break ups by trying to date Mr Perfect because he doesn't exist. Boyfriends are human like you and me. They make mistakes, do stupid things and can sometimes be really hurtful. If you search for someone who will always say and do the right thing, you're always going to be disappointed.

✳ If you go on a date and it's a disaster then go ahead and opt out. It's better to be honest than hang on, hoping for things to get better. Having said this, remember to give a new boyfriend a chance. He may not live up to your ex, or he may remind you of your ex, either way he's not your ex. There's nothing worse than being compared to somebody's ex-lover. It makes you feel insecure, jealous and annoyed. The past is the past and it's better off kept that way.

 FALLING IN LOVE AGAIN

Dating might feel fine for you but when it comes to love, you might think "No way – I'm never doing that again". Yet the chances are you will, and what's more, you'll be glad you did it. Love is tough but its good points outweigh its bad every time.

If you choose never to love again then you're missing out on some pretty wonderful experiences. Of course, it's going to hurt now and then, but it's also going to make you laugh, give you wonderful memories and make you very happy.

Good or bad, it will make you a stronger person. Happy or sad it will teach you more and more about yourself. And, for better or for worse, love really does make the world go round.